The Science of Solidarity

To Improve Personal Relationships,
Business Life, and Society

by

A. L. Ranen McLanahan, Ph.D.

© 2019 by A. L. Ranen McLanahan

All rights reserved. This book or any portion thereof may not be reproduced or used in any manner whatsoever without the express written permission of the publisher except for the use of brief quotations in a book review.

ISBN: 9781791681456

Table of Contents

Preface i
Chapter One 1
   Motivations 1
   What Is Solidarity? 5
Chapter Two 8
   The Solidarity Effect 8
   Setting Solidarity 11
   Brutal Consequences 15
   Solidarity on Humor 18
   Halo Effect 20
   Halo Effect on Trust 24
   Solidarity for Strangers 25
   The Solidarity Inheritance 29
   Summary of the Solidarity Effect 31
Chapter Three 32
   Building and Destroying Solidarity 32
   Solidarity's Golden Rule 35
   Solidarity through Respect 38
   Reciprocity, Hidden Values, and Soul-Crushing Guilt 41
   The Hidden Destruction of Solidarity 44
   The Dark Side of Trust and Respect 47
Chapter Four 53

- Solidarity Rule Sets for Personal Life and Business 53
- Interaction Rules 53
- Rule Sets That Will Destroy Marriages 56
- Rule Set: Value Awareness 61
- Rule Set: Be on Their Side 64
- Rule Set: Work with Reciprocity 67
- Rule Set: Observe Actions 71
- Rule Set: Reject Habitual Liars 75
- Rule Set: Rejoice in Honest Struggle 77

Chapter Five 80
- Solidarity and the World 80
- When We Make Cooperation Too Costly 82
- Solidarity Insanities 89
- Solidarity and the World 94
- Conclusions 97

Afterword 99

About the Author 100

References 101

Preface

"Why did you write this book?" It's a good question. I don't envy those who write. Being sequestered in a dark room, surrounded by stacks of other people's research, while friends and family have fun without you is probably a low human experience. Worse, if you care about what you're writing, the isolation can continue for years during revisions and rewrites. Why would anyone do this to themselves?

To put it simply, I didn't have a choice. I tried quitting this work many times, but I couldn't. Chapter 1 discusses some of my motivations, even big ones, but those alone weren't enough. The real reasons are tucked away in later chapters. I hope you'll understand better what I mean when we get there.

We're going to learn about the science of solidarity. As this work will suggest, solidarity is a far deeper concept than it first appears. I believe it has important applications for each of us in our personal and professional lives. It also has enormous ramifications for society and the world.

Perhaps this sounds like an exaggeration—something an editor would add to sell more books. I invite you to judge these claims yourself by book's end.

Chapter 1 introduces solidarity, why it matters, and what it is. It starts with a real-life story involving murderous intent. Chapter 2 is on the solidarity effect. We'll learn how solidarity completely changes how we are perceived by others. We'll see how the handsome can turn into the ugly, and the unattractive can transform into the glamorous. Chapter 3 discusses how solidarity rises and falls. It includes the hidden layers of solidarity that most of us are unaware of. Have you ever met someone who doesn't like you and you don't know why? We'll explore this and much more.

To help solidify concepts, chapter 4 is about applications. These include how solidarity can be used to deepen our friendships, create better relationships, and transform a workplace through our actions and choices. Chapter 5 explores solidarity in a larger context. It also contains some of the most devastating conclusions of this work.

Even though this book contains references, it isn't written to fellow academics; it's written to the rest of us. A major goal was to make this work's information understandable to as many people as possible. Why is this so important? Allow me to answer with a horrible quote from Pierre Bourdieu's seminal paper where social capital was first defined: "[Social capital is] the aggregate of the actual or potential resources which are linked to possession of a durable network of more or less institutionalized relationships of mutual acquaintance or recognition."

There are powerful ideas in Bourdieu's writing, but who would know other than the academics in his field? Historically, Bourdieu's own work was overlooked until enough understood its importance. If our words don't help a reader understand what we're saying, what use are they?

I don't know about you, but I feel a certain agony reading a large book built around a miserly amount of useful ideas. It always leaves me feeling empty and somewhat cheated. I've tried for the opposite extreme with this work. Each sentence, paragraph, and section were chosen intentionally and with a specific purpose in mind. I hope you'll find the result to be an extremely concise, filling read.

If I really care about solidarity's message, then clarity and concision aren't enough. I've learned from sad experience that boring an audience means an audience tuning out. When this happens, everyone's time is wasted. A message needs to be interesting. Maybe even entertaining when it can be. Fortunately for both of us, solidarity can be fascinating. It helps us understand others and ourselves on a deeper level, and it's a journey I'm excited to take with you.

Each chapter is steeped in real life stories. Some happened exactly as told. Others are compilations of true stories with minor reconstructions. These were made to protect people's privacy. We'll also use stories to explore historical examples and important research results. We'll do this by imagining you, the reader, are in an unnamed participant's shoes, getting to experience what they might have experienced.

Finally, who am I to write this book? I'm an engineer and teacher with some specialization in *performance management*. Just as importantly, I'm one of the 7.7 billion people on this Earth. When we don't understand solidarity's lessons, it can have high personal costs *for all of us*.

With all that said, we're ready to begin. We'll start with an "exactly as told" story about solidarity and murderous intent. See you in chapter 1.

-A. L. Ranen ("ray-nen") McLanahan,
        one of the 7.7 billion

Chapter One
Motivations

In my twenties, I worked on a floating factory ship in Alaska. The company I worked for had developed a machine that efficiently removed pin bones from fresh salmon. To test the machine, we put it on a floating factory ship and traveled to the cold, clear waters of Alaska for several months at a time. There, we'd buy fresh fish directly from the local fishermen and process them on the water.

I worked for this operation for several years. One thing I looked forward to each time was the food. Each year featured Alaska's oceanic bounty prepared in a medley of different ways. Occasionally, other ships donated other delicacies to our operation, including halibuts, giant tanner crabs, and the largest shrimp I've ever seen. Despite requiring long hours and months away from home, the venture was often a delicious one.

We'd bring in crew of several nationalities: Mexican, Taiwanese, Japanese, and American college student (American college students *felt* as if they were from their own country). Experience ranged from those starting out to lifelong processors jumping from one operation to the next. For months at a time, we'd hijack these workers away from their homes with promises of minimum wage, long hours, cramped conditions, and adventure. No alcohol or drugs were allowed on the ship, so, as I'm sure you suspect, there was a healthy bootlegging operation. (Full disclosure: I learned about the bootlegging late in my career. I probably seemed too stiff to be invited to the "fun." However, crew members telling one another they were "thirsty tonight" eventually tipped me off. Someone was getting a buzz, and it wasn't from ocean air).

Out at sea, the tight quarters made it impossible to get too far from anyone else, so people were expected to just get along. Teamwork, unity, and basic civility were as necessary as they were difficult to maintain. When things broke down, they broke down quickly. Coalitions among crew formed along racial lines. As one crew member told me about members of another race, "They are filth." I knew some on board thought the same about him.

Hatred among the crew could spread like a disease, sometimes to disastrous result. It seemed to spontaneously develop in a few and leap through the ship's physical barriers to affect more, while leaving others completely untouched. Why had it developed? How had it spread? Could anything be done about it, or was this just the way things were? I knew the stresses of the job didn't help; the long working hours, sharp fillet knives, and the tiny rectangular boxes we called bunks only caused tensions to further fray.

Speaking of fillet knives, fish processors had a special affinity with their knife. The knives on board had a comfortable, white-handled grip that sprouted an eight- to ten-inch blade ending in a wicked point. Processors depended on their knives to keep up on the processing line, and each was constantly honed until it could pull through the tough, armorlike scales of fish with minimal effort. Some processors brought their knives with them from operation to operation, sharpening them until the blade had retreated far in on itself, becoming a long, razorlike shank. For whatever reason, it was common to name them—for example, Excalibur, the Ram-Rod, El Death Weasel.

One year, our cook was on one side of the social divide. He was kind, but his cooking skills were less than desirable. He had an incomprehensible fondness for mushy, overcooked beans served with crunchy rice. This food was kept in large quantities for months at a time and was a staple of our voyage. (He also liked to serve fresh, deep-fried salmon with most lunches and dinners, but that's another story). However, he did run a tight galley and refused to let plates or utensils leave it. He didn't want them found later covered in unrecognizable growths. His no-plate-out-of-the-galley rule wasn't popular, and it caused some to complain loudly.

One afternoon, surrounded by group animosity and sharp knives, I collapsed in front of my lunch. It had been a long morning battling technical problems. As I dutifully shoveled calories into my mouth (more rice and beans!), I heard shouting in front of me. One of the processors was yelling across the galley at the cook. The cook stood immobile, his arms sternly folded across his wide chest. I wasn't sure what had started it, but I would hear later that the processor was trying, yet again, to bring his food to his room and get away from the rest of the "filth."

 The cook wouldn't yield, so the processor, having had his fill of feeling disrespected in public, lost it. With a scream, he ripped his processing knife away from his belt and rushed the cook.

 What happened next occurred fast. One of my friends, a man named Grant, leaped forward and tackled the processor to the ground. The processor brought the knife up to cut him, but he stopped before stabbing Grant. He continued to thrash wildly, though, trying to break free. When his knife was finally pulled out of his hands, he stopped struggling. All this happened on the floor mere feet from where I sat, my food still dangling on my fork as I watched in disbelief.

 The processor could have stabbed Grant. But he didn't. Earlier that season, Grant had been the processor's captain on one of the smaller ships and had earned his respect. When the processor was asked about it later, all he said was, "I didn't want to stab you, Captain. You are my friend."

 A violent breach in solidarity had caused the attack to start, but the strength of solidarity prevented further harm. In the aftermath, the processor was confined to his bunk with a civilian guard posted until the Coast Guard took him away. His breach in civility led him to prison and opened a darker chapter in his life. Grant was free to be an uninjured one-heck-of-a-guy. And our cook, his life spared, was free to undercook the rice and overcook the beans for the rest of the summer.

What Is Solidarity?

Solidarity is one of my favorite words in the English language. It's important to what we want to achieve, and I'd like to begin by defining it a few different ways.

Imagine you're watching your favorite sports team, whatever it is, making an absolutely brilliant play. As you watch this complex maneuver, each player seems to know what their team needs to do and what he or she must do in relation. There is a communication among players that transcends mere words alone and a trust that each will perform their role on time as needed. Once the play is successful, the thrill of what they just accomplished together is felt by players and spectators alike. This was something their opponents hadn't seen coming and had little defense against.

Maybe sports aren't your thing, and you're more of a music lover. You're at a concert to see one of your favorite bands play. This band has been together for years, and in that time, it's developed a performance cohesiveness that's exhilarating to watch. Its presence draws crowds from miles away.

Members of this band may play different instruments, but it's these unique differences that form the genius of their work. Take away a single instrument, or sometimes a single note, and the band's entire performance would suffer. Again, among players there is inherent trust that each will play their part on time and precisely as needed. As the band's complex harmony builds, the audience cheers. They love it, and the band knows it.

These are examples of human solidarity at its best. Solidarity speaks of the respect, trust, and understanding found within highly unified teams. Members have a place where they know their contributions are important, and their role is valued. Just being part of such a team brings a natural fulfillment, pride, and happiness that speaks to the deep human need within us all to belong to something great.

Although solidarity can form by itself, it can take years for the right people to find one another and develop the required level of trust. Even if the right people do find each other, chance and circumstance can prevent them from ever building something great together.

Here are two more very different reasons to care. The first is pure capitalism. For the shrewd business owner who measures human worth in dollars, a lack of solidarity means an unhappier workforce that is less motivated. This leads to more job hunts and retraining. New employees can take months to get to full working capacity, and they can still leave when job offers come from competitors. Further, when an employee leaves a company, they take today's most valuable commodity: information. Studies have shown that each salaried position can cost a company "1.5–2.0x the employee's annual salary" to replace. This includes the cost of "hiring, onboarding, training, ramp time to peak productivity, the loss of engagement from others due to high turnover, higher business error, and general culture impacts" [1]. There are many hard-line reasons to care about solidarity.

The second reason is from a human happiness perspective [2]. Most of us spend enormous amounts of time and life where we work. When a workplace is toxic, even slightly, unflattering interactions evolve. Interpersonal conflicts increase as people become more insecure, territorial, and reluctant to work together. As this continues, days are filled not with the joys and challenges of working together but with frustrations and insecurities. Simply said, without solidarity in an organization, the happiness of employees at all levels can be compromised, and a larger part of human life is spent in misery.

Annie Dillard once said, "How we spend our days is, of course, how we spend our lives." The time will pass either way. Whether we spend it building solidarity in our most important relationships or living far below our own potentials, the time will pass.

Solidarity. Noun. Union or fellowship arising from common responsibilities and interests, as among members of a group [3].

Chapter Two
The Solidarity Effect

"Why do we run box fans in our house in the summer?" I asked my thermodynamics class.

"Because it makes the air colder" was one reply. Nods came from other students.

I reworded the question. "Let's say you have a box fan in the middle of a closed room. The fan pulls two hundred watts from the wall socket, and the windows and doors are closed. Standing in front of the fan may make you *feel* cooler. But is it really making the air colder?"

Hesitation this time. "Um. Maybe?"

In reality, as much as it may feel colder, the air actually isn't. When the air isn't moving very quickly, we develop a plume of warmer air around us, and it acts like an invisible blanket. This blanket makes heat transfer more slowly from our skin. However, when we stand in front of a fan, much of that warm plume is blown away, and we lose heat faster.

Saying a fan makes the air colder seems right, and it *feels* right, but it's actually wrong. If you leave a two-hundred-watt fan running in a closed room, the air gains kinetic energy from the fan (think airspeed), but the air slows as it travels, and its kinetic energy becomes thermal energy. Over time, running a two-hundred-watt fan in a closed room is the same as running a two-hundred-watt heater. A fan makes the air feel colder as it really makes it warmer. It's one of many lessons the first law of thermodynamics teaches us.

OK. Why are we talking about this? It's because of what happened next.

After our class discussion, one student went home to tell their parents. Their parents often ran a fan in a closed room to "make the air colder." The student wanted to know what they thought of our lesson. Their parents *did* have thoughts and a message for me:

- They're right to run their fan; it makes the air colder.
- All that time in school has made me stupid.

I've met many types of parents. Some respect education and new ideas. Some do not. If I were to meet these parents to try and explain, how would the conversation go? They'd walk in with distrust and I with resentment. A conversation starting like this increases the chances that heads will butt, leaving all with migraines. Instead of progress, it's more likely we'd get wasted time.

But before I judge them as a lost cause, let's try an experiment. What might cause them to react the way they did?

I imagine these parents taught their kids the best they knew how. Like most parents, they want their children's trust and don't want to look foolish in front of them. Now, a small piece of their authority and tradition are threatened by an outsider. Moreover, the outsider's words seem really wrong. How could anyone say a fan makes air hotter? You can *feel* it do the opposite. And not only does this outsider contradict a lifetime of observation, they have also confused fans with heaters.

Under these conditions, there are two natural conclusions: (1) the outsider is wrong, and (2) for someone to make these kinds of mistakes, they must also be an idiot.

Further, if you later heard this "idiot" claiming a piece of wood from a freezer would feel warmer than a solid piece of metal from a refrigerator, then your idiot opinion would probably seem confirmed. Well, at least until you tried it for yourself. (If you do try this experiment, make sure the wood and metal are of similar size, kept dry, and have been in there at least a couple hours. Why does the metal feel so much colder when it's actually at a higher temperature? Humans don't feel temperature directly. We feel rates of heat transfer, and metals transfer heat more quickly than woods).

The world operates by many complex, seemingly contradictory rules. Sometimes the "obvious" is wrong. I can't blame others for making this kind of mistake. I've made it plenty myself. So if I were to meet these parents, I would now have new choices. Understanding could replace my earlier resentment. I'd be more willing to listen before speaking. When I did speak, it could be with more patience. That would raise my possibility of being understood. In the language of this book, by raising my solidarity with them, I would increase the chances that they actually hear me.

We'll define level of solidarity for another person or group as the general level of trust, respect, and understanding we have for them. As we'll see, when solidarity for another changes, it sets off a cascade of automatic reactions within the brain. Some of the consequences are obvious, but many are not. In this chapter, watch how someone's level of solidarity completely changes how another is perceived.

High Solidarity	Low Solidarity
Our missteps seem understandable	Our successes seem threatening
Our troubles seem relatable	Our jokes seem less funny
Our physiques seem attractive	Our personalities seem less attractive
Our jokes seem funnier	Our faults seem more acute
Our successes seem more gratifying	Our failures seem more exaggerated

Setting Solidarity

I'd like to introduce you to Teddy, a healthy six-month-old infant. He's pretty amazing. He's learned the usual tricks of his age. He can roll. He can recognize people familiar to him. He can mostly sit up without support (and when Teddy tips over while gnawing on a stuffed animal's ear, it's in that adorable slow motion only babies can manage). When you smile at Teddy, he gets excited. If you look sad, Teddy droops. He can't crawl yet, but he's a scooting fiend. Here comes Teddy! Teddy's hungry! Teddy wants to chew on power cords! (The house now needs more Teddy proofing.)

You enroll Teddy in a study on infants. In the study, Teddy sits on your lap while cameras track his attention. In front of you is a puppet show.

The curtain draws back, revealing a small block puppet with enormous googly eyes that roll around when it moves. Like all puppets in this show, it doesn't speak or have other facial features. We'll call this first googly-eyed puppet Climber.

Climber is at the bottom of Puppet Mountain. Climber makes a brave attempt to reach the summit, working its way up the slope. However, near the top, Climber finds misadventure. Climber can't make it and slides back down Puppet Mountain. It's just too steep.

Fortunately, another block puppet appears at the bottom of the mountain. It's a different color, but it has similar googly eyes. We'll call this block Ally. When Climber tries again, Ally helps, giving Climber little boosts until Climber reaches the top. Success! Filled with the joy of puppet mountaineering, Climber does a little "dance" hopping from one of its little blocky "feet" to the other. The curtain closes.

When the curtain opens again, Climber is back on the ground, and it again attempts to climb the mountain.

Will Climber make it this time? No—as before, Climber can't make it and slides down. Undaunted, our brave hero tries again. However, this time, a third googly-eyed block appears at the top of the mountain. We'll call this one Rival. Rival gets in Climber's way and gives him small, rough shoves back down the mountain. Puppet betrayal of the worst kind! Again, the curtain falls.

Teddy, like other infants in this study, watches the show with wide-eyed interest. It's pretty obvious what he's thinking. Best. Television. Ever! The two shows repeat until Teddy loses interest, as measured by his eye contact.

After the shows, researchers bring out Ally and Rival spaced equally apart on a tray. They put them in front of Teddy. It's been shown infants will reach for things they like, and researchers want to know which block will Teddy reach for.

Here things get really interesting. Teddy can't talk, crawl, or sit reliably without support. He's an infant of many sounds but practically no words. Can he understand, at any level, the dynamics of interpersonal relationships? Does he comprehend what he saw? Does he even care? After all, if infants don't understand what they've watched, then we'd expect a fifty-fifty distribution between infants choosing Ally and Rival, assuming they reached for either.

However, that's not what happens. Teddy, like the other 100 percent of infants tested, chooses Ally [4]. Additionally, although infants looked at both blocks, they spent far less time looking at Rival compared to Ally.

Rival had somehow become unworthy of their six-month-old time.

What was going on in Teddy's mind? It's doubtful he had a long internal dialogue before making his choice. It's more likely that when Teddy looked at Ally, he *felt* drawn to it, as if the act of cooperation had made Ally a much more interesting block somehow. In the language of this book, Ally had earned a higher solidarity with Teddy than Rival had. And it affected the infant's choice. *And he's only six months old.*

Want to go deeper? Researchers repeated their study using three-month-old infants. What was Teddy able to do at this age? He was working to hold his head steady without wobbling too much. He wasn't mobile, but he would try by kicking when placed on his stomach. He'd also reach for objects and put them in his mouth. (Teddy was still hungry, after all!)

Infants this young have unreliable motor skills. Cameras recorded how long infants looked at each block and which one they reached for [5] [6]. With their brains in such early development, what would a group of three-month-olds choose? Would we see a fifty-fifty split?

If Teddy had been tested at this age, he might have done what the other 100 percent of three-month-olds did. All reached out for Ally [7]. On average, they looked at Rival half as long as they did Ally before making this choice. Rival somehow wasn't worth more of their precious three-month-old attention.

What happened when the infants studied were given the choice between Ally and Climber instead of

Rival? Ally was chosen more often than Climber. What happened when the choice was between Climber and Rival instead of Ally? Climber was chosen more often.

There is a hopeful message in this. Long before language, fine motor controls, or even the muscular strength required to hold our heads steady have developed, most of us are drawn to cooperation. In other studies, those who lack these basic social tendencies are also more psychopathic, which may be caused by the way their brains have formed [8] [9] [10].

So at three months old (and possibly younger), most babies have a strong, intuitive understanding of solidarity. They remember, at least for a while, acts of kindness and feel drawn to them. And perhaps most hopeful for humankind, they overwhelmingly reject cruelty.

But it doesn't stay that way.

Brutal Consequences

Imagine you've been invited to play a win-some-money, get-some-shocks research game with two other participants. In the win-some-money part, you take turns sending your cash to other players. When you do, the cash multiplies. Other players can then send their cash back, causing it to multiply further. Over several rounds, the more cash players send, the more cash there is to win.

The first player (whom we'll call Ally) sends you a fair sum. You send a fair amount back. You both have more money than when you started. However, when you send the third player money, they send little back.

What happened here? Doesn't this person understand the rules? We'll call this other player Rival. Round after round, Ally continues to cooperate with you, but Rival does not. At the end of the game, you do have more money than when you started, but not as much as you could have.

Now for the get-some-shocks part. You fill out a quick survey about other players. Then each of you gets placed in a separate functional magnetic resonance imaging (fMRI) machine. These machines measure activity throughout your brain. In the machine, one of your hands is positioned so it's on camera. A small video screen shows you the hands of all three participants.

One at a time, each of your hands gets an electric shock. Your hand gets zapped. (Ouch.) You watch Ally's hand get zapped. You watch Rival's hand get zapped.

After a few rounds of shocks, you're released from the machine, given the cash you won, and told what was going on.

In this game, researchers weren't interested in Ally or Rival. Both were actors. They were interested in you. The fMRI machine measured what was going on in your brain when you watched the other players get shocked [11].

Ally had developed higher solidarity with players. When players watched Ally's hand get shocked, areas of the brain associated with empathy spiked. As recorded through direct measurement of the brain, people saw Ally's pain partly as theirs.

However, when Rival's hand was shocked, something different happened. First, activity to people's empathy centers didn't spike. For some participants, it even decreased. Participants didn't say to themselves, "I'm going to turn off activity to my empathy centers in my brain right when this person's hand is shocked so I won't have to feel this person's pain." Instead, the brain automatically did this for them without their conscious choice. It wouldn't allow them to see, feel, or experience Rival's pain the same way as Ally's.

Further, when Rival was shocked, some participants had activity spike in their brain's reward center. For these participants, watching another human in pain was rewarding. Again, this wasn't a conscious choice. No one says, "At the exact instant of the shock, I'm going to activate the reward center of my own brain while watching the suffering of another human." Again, the brain does this automatically without conscious thought or deliberation.

Deeper still, players filled out a survey before the shock session to rate Ally and Rival. In the survey, Rival was perceived to be more aggressive, more unlikeable, and less physically attractive.

Did it take much for these two polar-opposite perceptions to set in? No. Short interactions can dramatically move the mind's needle. It's automatic. Once we decide we don't like someone else, for any reason, the rest of the brain gets on board, shutting off our empathy while giving us hits of rewarding dopamine when we see them fail. It's what our brains do without our realizing it. This is the state of low solidarity for another.

Solidarity on Humor

What if high solidarity could make you funnier? As we'll see, it makes all the difference.

First, is it really jokes that make people laugh? Researchers tested this by listening to groups of friends. These groups laughed freely, and researchers wanted to know why. What they found was counterintuitive. Most laughter came from things an outsider wouldn't find funny [12].

I started paying attention to this. Here's a sample of lines that, in my own groups, got laughs:

- "That's so you."
- "Sorry, it's getting late."
- "That's a 'Ranen-ism' for sure."
- "I need to get back to work."
- "The drag coefficient of my truck is 0.42."

I'd say you had to be there to understand the laugh, but it isn't enough. None of these was a punchline. For example, I was asked to take some pictures of a group of my students for a competition. I took some. When I was done, I said, "Yep, those are some pictures." Laughter.

It isn't so much what's said. The laughter also comes from the camaraderie. After all, if someone else doesn't know, or doesn't care, what it's like to be you, how can sentences like "Yep, those are some pictures" be laugh-out-loud funny?

Comedians discuss this phenomenon. One rule is to connect with their audience as early as possible. For example, in *Why Do I Do This?* Bill Burr starts with a bit on crowd numbers and free tickets before saying he didn't do anything all day. "I'm serious. I'm a loser, man. I sat around watching TV and all kinds of stuff" [13]. These are things his audience can understand and relate to, and it might make the rest of his routine funnier because of it.

Comedian Ian Harris discussed this further. In his early career, the exact same routine with the same timing could "kill it" on one night with big laughs. The next, it would "eat it" with little audience reaction. He realized it wasn't just words and timing that make jokes work. There is something in audience connection that's vital. And when an audience doesn't connect with a comedian, even mildly risky material can cause offense, complaints, and walkouts.

Instead of leaving this to chance, he began purposely engaging his audience as early as possible. Once he felt them "following him," he'd use riskier jokes with far more potential to offend. This led to even bigger laughs. Astoundingly, with the same audience, he'd watch a fellow comedian use less offensive material and get the same audience's pushback [14].

It's not words that offend alone. It's also the regard we have for the person behind the words. When someone connects with another, solidarity rises, and faults become understandable while offenses become overlookable.

Maybe you can think of a friend or family member who illustrates this. Do you know someone whose mouth runs but doesn't mean harm? Someone about whom you say, "I see how others would find this person offensive, but if you actually knew him or her, you wouldn't be offended." If you do, you've felt this part of solidarity. It's the leniency we grant those we know and understand. When our solidarity for them is high enough, this comes naturally.

Conversely, low solidarity has ugly consequences. As solidarity drops, the audience feels the comedian is no longer on their side. They feel more justified interrupting them, booing them, or shouting over their words. Whereas someone would never throw an object at another under any other circumstance, low solidarity emboldens this action. The audience no longer sees the speaker as a fellow human. Instead, low solidarity transforms the speaker into an inconvenient obstacle to be overcome. When audience members are asked later, justifications come quickly. They say the speaker "shouldn't have run their mouth" and "just had it coming." These justifications leave little room for remorse.

Halo Effect

If you needed to leave your purse, wallet, child, and/or other valuables with a stranger for a day, and you only knew their profession, who would you feel most comfortable with? A doctor? A street performer? An officer? An accountant? A Wall Street investor? A bartender? A priest? Someone else? Is there a profession you'd feel completely comfortable with?

Would more details about this person change your choice? Would you prefer someone richer or poorer?

Younger or older? Male or female? Pink, yellow, white, black, tan, olive, green, or blue skinned? Religious or irreligious? Straight, LGBTQ, or still deciding?

Finally, is there some combination you'd trust most? For example, a poor, religious female accountant of European descent who is LGBTQ? Or a rich, irreligious male police officer of mixed cultural heritage who is straight? Feel free to mix and match to make yourself as comfortable as you can with your choice.

No matter the combination, this is still a stranger we're talking about. Yet without knowing more about them than some labels, we can find combinations we're more comfortable with and ones we'd never feel comfortable about.

Often, we don't know more than another's general appearance and most obvious set of traits. Yet from this alone, our solidarity for them can dramatically, and actionably, start higher or lower. That is, our level of trust, willingness to understand, and regard for their well-being will change based on the most obvious things we know about them. Let's look at facts:

- In general, the physically attractive make more money than the unattractive for the same job [15].
- Well-behaved students are seen as more intelligent by their teachers, even when they're not [16].
- Attractive criminals get softer sentences for the same crime [17].
- Enthusiastic employees are rated higher than they really are in areas having nothing to do with enthusiasm [18].

Or in general:
- A defining trait in one area dramatically changes how that person is viewed in unrelated areas [19].

Collectively, this is known as the halo effect. What we don't know about a person is greatly influenced by what we do, even if they are quickly assigned labels. This can work either for or against us. When judged by others, our most defining feature is the lens through which our unknown qualities are viewed. The effect is actionable. It can compel actions either for or against us that people would never otherwise consider.

For example, consider independent filmmaker Andy Laub, who documented hiking the Pacific Crest Trail with his friend. The trail is 2,659 miles long and stretches from the Mexican border to Canada. It is a major undertaking attempted by the determined, the adventurous, and those who can afford the gear, meals, and a six-month break from a job.

Their journey started with immediate problems. They initially packed food for a two-thousand-calorie diet but found hiking with heavy loads all day burned far more. Their learning curve made hiking companions out of various human miseries: coldness, hunger, exhaustion, sunburns, thirst, bug bites, and homesickness. However, with determination to finish, they pushed on. Hair and beards grew with the journey.

After months of concentrated effort, their spirits needed a lift. Independence Day approached, which held deep meaning for them on their journey. The pair considered how to best commemorate this. They decided to temporarily hitchhike away from the trail to celebrate with fellow Americans on the California coast. It took some days, but they managed to reach the coast just in time. They refreshed themselves, stopped at a convenience store to purchase flags, and hit the beach in anticipation of festivities. "Surrounded by thousands of holiday beachgoers, we hadn't seen so many people since leaving [home]…We made a toast to Independence Day, the birthday of our freedom."

However, it's here the camera cuts out. The pair reappears walking in darkness away from the beach. Their enthusiasm is replaced with frustration and sad acceptance. It seems the town's locals didn't approve of the pair's backpacks and long hair. They were mistaken for wandering vagrants and run out of town [20].

This is the halo effect in action. It doesn't matter how talented, charismatic, or intelligent this pair of adventurers was. Their most outward trait was their long hair and backpacks. It made people so uncomfortable that their other characteristics were automatically assumed. With what I'd guess to be righteous indignation, locals forced these perceived unwantables off public land so they could go back to celebrating their holiday in peace.

The halo effect has major consequences for all of us. Our most defining traits matter. Do we know what they are for ourselves? Is the first thing people notice something positive? Is it our friendliness, our tidy appearance, our confidence, or another positive trait? Or is it our boredom, our worries, our unhappiness, or a different negative trait? This affects how the rest of our traits are assumed. It will change how others see our honesty, reliability, and trustworthiness. It will change their ability to see our struggles as theirs. By the small things, another's solidarity for us raises or lowers. When it does, it takes their perception of us with it.

Let's see an example of this.

Halo Effect on Trust

A stranger comes to your door, interrupting dinner, relaxation, or family time. The stranger asks you to listen to them talk. Then they request your name, credit card number, and other sensitive personal information, such as your cell phone number and email address. They assure you they are only going to use this information in a way you will approve of.

Would you give this to them?

From a purely mechanical point of view, people give out this information in this circumstance all the time. Years ago, my friend did a stint as a door-to-door salesman selling pesticide treatments. His company had an entire training regimen for what he was to do at the door. He was to appear in his company's crisp uniform. It was never to be wrinkled or stained. He was to stand with confidence and speak with as much of the company's approved language (that is, professional selling points) as possible. He was never to do anything that could be construed as unprofessional.

Because his job was commission based, he needed to interrupt as many people as possible each day, get them to listen to him, and make the sale by collecting credit card information. He became the company's best salesman for a time, too. How? He mastered a small part of the halo effect. He focused on coming across as caring, concerned, and professional. When people saw his most obvious traits as positive, they assumed his unknown level of honesty, integrity, and trustworthiness must be high as well. Ten minutes later, he'd make the sale and move on to the next house.

One of his customers commented on the strangeness of it. "I feel weird handing out personal information to a complete stranger. I usually don't do this. However, there is something about you that I think I can trust." He did this because his unknown characteristics were assumed through his most visible one's. Trust rose, solidarity rose, and requests that should be impossible became daily bread.

Solidarity for Strangers

In a town, I came upon an SUV flipped over on its hood by an intersection. Around the wreckage, a self-directed and self-organized community of strangers rushed to help. Some stood in the street directing traffic around the accident. Some went to aid passengers, while others went to the driver. Another paced on the sidewalk calling in emergency services. None of them said, "Well, that looks bad, but I've got other places to be." No, they felt compelled to help as if the victims were their own friends and family.

Most people have a certain medium level of solidarity for strangers. Our brains allow us to feel their suffering even when it's uncomfortable to us [21]. But there is more to it.

About a year before, I spotted a similar accident in a large city. However, no one stopped. Instead, people drove on, offering nothing to victims but stares. If this scene of suffering affected them, it wasn't actionable. Why the difference?

Before exploring this, let's look at a more dramatic example. On January 12, 2010, Haiti experienced a 7.0 magnitude earthquake. In seconds, people's lives, businesses, and property were visited by devastation. An estimated one hundred thousand died, with even more injured. How did the world respond? Did it just drive on? Not this time. Jeremy Rifkin, in the production *The Empathic Civilisation*, said it best: "Within an hour the tweeters came out, and within two hours some cell-phone videos [appeared on] YouTube, and within three hours the entire human race was in an empathic embrace coming to the aid of Haiti." The world united as with one voice to say, "Hold on, we're coming" [22].

The Haiti disaster compelled people of different religions, genders, politics, and ethnicities to act for a group of strangers they didn't know and would probably never meet. They did it, at least for this disaster, because how could they not? Haiti's suffering was, in some way, happening to them.

However, many disasters don't capture the world's attention. Sometimes we feel compelled to help. Sometimes we do not. Why?

First, when we're stressed, we're less likely to feel another's pain. A stressed brain disallows its user much empathy [23], and this seems to temporarily lower solidarity for everyone around. It can make someone snap at friends and family. It can make someone unfriendly with their clients. It can make bosses take out frustrations on employees they otherwise like and respect.

It may have affected reactions to the two different car accidents. The stressful environment of the large city may have changed what the brain would allow drivers to feel about another's suffering. Without a driver's conscious permission, empathy was dulled, and the same accident caused a completely different response.

Second, understanding is important. Haiti disaster videos became widely available. It was well covered by the news. Stories of individuals who lost everything circulated. When we understand another, their troubles become more real to us. It turns an unknown person in some country we may never visit into an injured mother desperately searching for her only child or a father trying to get medical help for his dying wife.

This power can't be overstated. Understanding can rapidly change how we feel about another and how others feel about us. For example, imagine you've been waiting in line when someone pushes in front of you. As you watch, they continue shoving their way to the front. Why couldn't they wait in line like everyone else? What makes them so special? What a jerk, right?

However, what if you learned this person was trying to reach their friend who was having a seizure? Suddenly, things are different. I've been in a similar situation. Understanding transformed my anger into asking how I could help in the span of heartbeats.

Third, our anxieties about another matter. When anxiety falls and we understand another's struggles, the differences between us become less important [24] [25]. For example, during the height of the American gay-marriage debate, those against it said it would degrade the entire institute of marriage. They cited their strong moral concerns and the possible downfall of America.

Whatever our views on this may be, let's see the role anxiety and understanding played in public opinion. Gallup polls found those who knew someone in the LGBTQ community were more likely to support the movement [26]. Over the years, as more of the LGBTQ community felt comfortable coming forward, more of the public knew someone, and national anxieties fell.

Let's go back to Haiti's disaster. Let's say, for some reason, the world mistakenly feared Haiti's people and saw them as a threat. Then, when the earthquake hit, would the response have been different? Would more have seen the disaster as a good fortune that crippled a perceived threat? Would this have caused some to even celebrate the exact same event?

This is the tragedy of misplaced anxiety. It destroys all potential for empathy and basic decency. For some, it can turn tragedy into celebration.

Our takeaway is that anxiety lowers solidarity. When anxiety is misplaced, it causes additional untold injustices. Our own brains transform an injured mother trying to find her only child back into an unknown person in a country we don't plan to visit. And when we see others as a threat for any reason, even if they're not, solidarity for them lowers, making their suffering seem less urgent.

This leads us into our last, darkest main result of the chapter.

The Solidarity Inheritance

If someone, or some group, decides they don't like you, it doesn't matter how charismatic, intelligent, or successful you really are. All they see is how flawed, unworthy, and undesirable you are to them. It doesn't matter if they are wrong. To them, you're no longer perceived as human as everyone else. Your pain means less. Your failures feel satisfying. And with this, we're ready to look at one of the bleakest parts of human nature. Want to better understand racism, misogyny, bigotry, and discrimination? The solidarity effect explains it succinctly.

It takes little to lower solidarity. If our parents, politics, religion, or peers teach us that another gender, religion, orientation, political ideology, or ethnicity is fundamentally wrong, sick, perverse, or evil, we start with a low level of solidarity for that group. Their other unknown qualities are assumed through the halo effect. We have more anxiety about the role they play in our society, which pushes solidarity down further. We stop perceiving them as fellow humans struggling through life the same as everyone else.

History has shown us that humans are capable of incredible levels of compassion. However, this doesn't extend to groups we've learned to despise. Our brains automatically close off the normal pathways that otherwise would bind us together as fellow humans. At a low enough level, their pain becomes meaningless, their appeals to humanity unintelligible, and their presence unwanted. Even if they are, in all other ways, the same as us. If someone tries to argue on their behalf, we feel they are deceived, confused, or are an idiot who can't see what's so "obviously" felt. Instead of listening to their entreaties, we start thinking of all the reasons we're right, further entrenching ourselves in our own position.

Every interaction we have with members of this other group is colored by our own negative perception. It's hard to see them any other way because, fundamentally, the human brain wants to believe what it already believes, especially when those beliefs are foundational to our worldview. Information that challenges our view feels like further inconveniences that can be justifiably ignored.

Unless someone actively wants to expand their worldview, counterfacts aren't sought. So, when we feel we could be wrong about another group, we seek reassurances from sources that will tell us what we want to hear. We listen to radio programs, podcasts, and news sources that will confirm what we already believe, and because the news source feels like it's on our side, our solidarity with the source grows. If someone calls out a source for using bad data, shoving its own agenda on us, or promoting biased views, it doesn't register with us because it feels like they are attacking one of our allies. The outsider's words can't be heard because we're too busy coming up with rebuffs against the attacker.

So, safely cocooned in our biased notions, we are free to spread them to our friends through daily conversations. Over time, our friends spread the bias to their friends and on to their children, who never have a chance to see things differently. In this way, it's the natural order for misunderstanding and misinformation to spread through a society like a disease, siphoning the social forces that would otherwise hold its people true to each other.

This is, perhaps, the bleakest part of solidarity. Can anything be done? We'll look at potential solutions in upcoming chapters. Until then:

Summary of the Solidarity Effect

We've seen that our level of solidarity is automatically set by our background, current believes, and daily interactions with other people. Higher levels act as a binding force holding our most important relationships together. It can make us more relatable, more forgivable, better looking, and funnier. Lower solidarity transforms us from fellow humans into obstacles unworthy of another's time or empathy.

Chapter Three
Building and Destroying Solidarity

One of my students was working as an intern on a factory floor. After a few months, he saw many small changes that could improve the speed and quality of the company's processes. In other words, this company had hired an intern who cared. I've had interns like this working for me. They're a type that continuously adds value to whatever project they're assigned.

However, the intern made a youthful mistake. Instead of discussing his ideas with the plant manager, who was only intermittently on the floor, he gathered his fellow workers together before a shift. He told them about his ideas and led them in making changes.

The intern wondered how anyone could complain. The company's goal was efficiency, and if anyone could make things run better, that should be valued. And if he managed to make their lines run faster with reduced waste, he'd prove he was a valuable hire. These were the types of thoughts that filled the intern's head. As the shift wore on, his excitement grew.

However, like so many before him, he hadn't considered an important aspect of human nature.

A plant manager is a weighty position. The manager knows how many thousands (and sometimes tens of thousands) of dollars an hour it costs when production is interrupted. They are aware of big picture concerns such as how a single part being off by a tenth of a millimeter can make later assembly impossible. To reach peak operation, they seek a Goldilocks zone where everything comes together just right and all the mechanical problems, scheduling snags, supply flow delays, and human-element issues are kept below a critical threshold.

Just as importantly, a manager needs their employees' trust. They can't afford to look foolish in their eyes.

As the plant manager made his nightly walk-through, it became apparent that his authority and established processes had been compromised. His pace through the floor increased. Who had authorized these changes? Who would have such blatant disrespect for him and his role? Didn't these people know that processes exist for a reason? Didn't they know what would happen if they were to have a single faulty run of products? A recall could mean everyone losing their job.

The more he saw, the angrier he got. He stopped the production run, shouting profanity. Who was responsible for this? The other workers sheepishly pointed him to the intern. His anger exploded at the intern in shrill words that could be heard through the factory's walls and out in the parking lot.

Aftermath: the intern quit. It was a year later when I heard his story, and he was still bad-mouthing the company he had once been excited to improve. He warned my other students away from working for this company and talked loudly about the problems with their products. As far as he knew, all his changes had been immediately discarded by "the idiots in charge."

To the yeller, it might feel good to vent their disappointment and frustration on another, even if regret follows later. It's a short-term gain with long-term consequences. When directed at someone else, it communicates, quite clearly, that you're not on their side, don't value their contributions, and don't think what they are doing is important. When done in front of others, it shames and embarrasses. This causes a rapid destruction of solidarity.

The ex-intern's embarrassment at how he had been treated was raw even a year later. His story was told from his perspective, and since he was well liked, it enlisted sympathy. It didn't matter that the intern had made a mistake. That part was mostly lost in his telling. However, the company's reputation continued to take damage with each retelling as more people became his coalition of sympathizers.

Let's rewind a year. What would happen if the plant manager had done everything the same but without the yelling and profanity? What if he had been more understanding of his intern's youthful enthusiasm? What if he had explained the possible dangers of the intern's actions?

Then there would have been room for a conversation. The intern might have learned a valuable lifelong lesson. The plant manager might have seen his operation through fresh eyes. And just possibly, the entire company might have been strengthened.

Through solidarity, a small difference could have changed entire trajectories. Let's see further mechanisms that raise and lower solidarity.

Solidarity's Golden Rule

If there is a golden rule for building solidarity, it's "be on their side." When we feel someone is looking out for our interests, solidarity with them grows. Even in situations that should lead to conflict, we can be on the other person's side and build solidarity anyway. Every interaction provides opportunity. This can be done without being a yes-person or letting others push you around. In fact, solidarity can build even as you assert your own interests.

Let's illustrate with a story. My wife and I bought our first home in 2011. It was a great space for children, but it came with a backyard full of an invasive species called buckthorn. Buckthorn is an aggressive, fast-growing tree that becomes covered in what I like to call "impale thorns." We did most cutting and destumping ourselves over sweat-soaked summers and blistery winters. It took seven years. And naturally, the week we reached our back fence, we received an easement request from the city across its entire width.

The easement would mean we'd lose property rights. We'd be limited in what we could plant, build, or do with that part of our property. If we wanted to build or plant, we'd need to request an encroachment to use our own land. Further, the easement would stay with the property forever, potentially lowering its value. The city offered no compensation.

After some research, I learned refusing an easement could bring legal complications in the form of eminent domain. If that happened, we could be taken to court by the city and forced to give them land rights. It's a situation with a high potential for conflict.

However, let's see what happens when we constantly, and openly, try building solidarity where we can. At first, it might seem that being on their side means just giving them what they want. However, nothing is further from truth. Being a pushover is not part of building solidarity. Conversely, being aggressively assertive can lower it. "Us versus them" comes naturally, but it tends to make problems for both "us" and "them."

So how can solidarity build when people's goals are diametrically opposite? How can conflict resolve to everyone's best interest? Each situation is different, but the principle is the same. Be on their side.

We needed the easement agent to look out for us, just as we'd look out for them. This wouldn't happen by pretending to be something we're not. But it could happen through a willingness to understand, respect, and openly support our shared values. When we do this for others, they tend to do the same in return. *This is the key that makes all the difference.*

I asked myself what it would be like as an easement agent. How many angry homeowners must they deal with each week? How refreshing would it be for a homeowner to be more interested in listening than angrily complaining?

When I called the easement agent, I greeted him as I would a new friend. I was uneasy about the request, and I didn't try to hide this. Still, I called to listen and understand. He talked, and I looked for what he said that I could support. During our conversation, we established the following:

- Easements like these provide services for the entire community.
- What he was trying to do was important.
- Easements should ask only for things that are necessary, nothing more.

So having acknowledged the importance of what he was trying to do, I felt I understood him. Just as importantly, I believe he felt understood. Now, it was my turn, so I briefly described our buckthorn labor years and our plans for the back property the easement would dismantle.

He agreed to drive over and discuss further. When he arrived, I again greeted him as I would a new friend. We talked about easements, the difficulties of his job, and the importance of finding solutions with the community.

He came with construction plans so I could better see what they were trying to do.

However, as he explained the plans, I noticed they had an easement on the other side of our fence. The one they had requested would help construction, but it was also redundant. We had established property owners should give up only what was necessary. Nothing more. And in this case, a new easement wasn't strictly necessary. I asked him if he thought it fair to give up property rights and lower property value when it wasn't really essential.

After a short discussion, he saw things from our perspective and retracted the request.

Because we were willing to be on his side, he was willing to be on ours. There was no arguing. There was no ongoing legal battle. There was no agreement to anything unreasonable. Instead, there was a special solidarity-building assertiveness.

Be on the other person's side, and they may try to be on yours in return. This is something we'll return to in future examples.

Solidarity through Respect

There is one more fundamental concept we need before taking things deeper. Imagine you've been invited to play a game of ball with others who have the same skill as you. At first, everything seems fine. They pass the ball to you, and you pass it back. Over time something changes. They start passing you the ball less and less, even when you're open. After a while, they stop including you completely. You've been playing just as well as everyone else. For reasons unknown, they're now actively ignoring you. Why?

This scenario was used by a research group on unsuspecting participants. The participants were brought into separate rooms to play a computer game of catch online while having their brains scanned. However, instead of playing online with other humans, they were really playing the game offline with computer AIs [27].

At first, the AIs passed the ball around to both other AIs and the human player. During the last third of the game, the AI started only passing the ball to other AIs.

Human players, feeling their peers were suddenly shutting them out, experienced a dramatic change in their brain's activity. An area of the brain associated with physical pain began pulsing with electricity. It was responding in a similar way as when there is physical injury. "Immediate problem! This can't continue! Do something!"

It's been said that disrespect is pain, and by direct measurement of the brain, this statement isn't wrong. Most of us know what this is like. Has someone ever yelled at you? Belittled you? Criticized you repeatedly for your perceived faults? Shamed you in front of peers? These kinds of acts feel painful for a reason.

For solidarity, disrespect says another person isn't on your side, doesn't value what you contribute, and might think little of your worth as a fellow human. They may not mean these things, but it doesn't matter. It's not about what's meant. It's about how it's perceived. When we do this to others, it can cause the rapid destruction of solidarity. With it comes its host of negative consequences.

If disrespect exists in an environment, solidarity can only rise with great difficulty. Showing respect, on the other hand, shows another person that they have value. This can raise solidarity. How can you show another person respect? Here's a small, partial list:

- Remembering another person's name and something about them
- Really listening to another person instead of just waiting for your turn to speak
- Asking other people for their opinions and taking their ideas seriously
- Treating other people like they have value to add to a conversation, project, or decision
- Looking out for someone else's interests as if they were your own
- Celebrating other people's successes
- Empathizing with their setbacks
- Speaking well of people to others, even when they're not around
- Complimenting good ideas other people have when you hear them
- Treating others as fellow humans and not like objects
- Being happy to see others when you meet them

If you're trying to build solidarity with someone this way, don't fake it. If someone picks up on insincerity, they can label the offender as a deceiver and manipulator, lowering solidarity. Worse, once someone sees your actions as dishonest, it's the lens through which they view all your future words and actions.

But if you can learn to genuinely like the people around you and then demonstrate respect for them in your own small ways, solidarity can build over time.

The takeaway is easy to summarize. Disrespect is pain. Disrespect destroys solidarity. To build solidarity and help an organization reach greater heights, the consequences of disrespect must be understood and its occurrences called out.

Reciprocity, Hidden Values, and Soul-Crushing Guilt
This letter came to Carlotta Flores, a longtime restaurant owner:

> I worked for you as a waitress very briefly back in the 1990's while a student at U of A. One of the waiters I worked with had encouraged me to "forget" to ring in a few drinks a shift and pocket the cash. And for some stupid reason, I did it…Thankfully, I was a terrible waitress and you all fired me before it could amount to more than a few hundred dollars total. It's been 20 years, but I still carry great remorse. I am very sorry that I stole from you. Please accept my apology [and] this money as repayment.

It contained $1,000 in cash. When she shared this letter with her restaurant's managers, they felt for the sender's decades of regret. Some were moved to tears.

Flores didn't know who this individual was. "We're usually a first-time employer for a young person being away from home and going to school...It's a good feeling to know that she felt she needed to take care of this, and I really respect her for it. If I knew her or saw her, I think I would give her a hug and tell her thank you whether or not [the letter included] the money."

In this, we have a powerful act driven by something deep from within. Maybe the person who did the wrong was the only one who knew about it—but that can be enough. In this example, it caused someone decades of agony until she finally made it right. Somewhere deep within the brain itself are cognitive forces that can overpower selfishness. The effect it produces is called reciprocity, and it's described as one of the great social powers that hold society together [28] [29]. Without conscious thought or permission, our brain dutifully logs rights and wrongs in the areas we care about [30].

Maybe you've felt something similar about a past harm you've caused—something that writhes against your sense of integrity until you finally make amends (or until you find enough self-justifications to feel inaction is acceptable). No one says to themselves, "Remember that time I acted against my own morals? I'm going to activate parts of my brain that make me feel terrible until I can't take it anymore and right this imbalance." Or if someone does us wrong, we don't say, "I'm going to activate regions that make me resentful and constantly remind me of the imbalance between us. I'll only turn it off again when I feel this person has paid for it somehow." Instead, it just happens, especially in the areas we individually value most.

Not everyone has the same level of these senses in all things. Take the real-life example of Ken and John. John was a longtime thief. He placed no value on the rights of ownership, at least when it came to other people. He could steal with no sense of regret or soul-crushing shame. Reciprocity held no sway over him or his actions in this area.

The area John did care about was social currency. He loved the way possessions could make him appear more sophisticated and respectable. Being seen as sophisticated was something that mattered a great deal to John. He'd notice it in others, and he wanted more for himself. To pass up stealing was to pass up an opportunity to have more of what he cared about. Perhaps the only thing he would feel regret for was a missed opportunity. One of his favorite things to steal was rare and expensive books.

In complete contrast to John was Ken, a bookseller endowed with a powerful sense of fair play. It was an area of high reciprocity for him, and because of this, he felt book theft was "an almost personal attack on him." When it started happening habitually to his fellow booksellers, Ken didn't feel right doing nothing. The repeated robberies lighted a fire within him, and he felt compelled to act. He systematically conducted interviews, followed leads, and tracked down the thief. Ultimately, Ken identified John to the police [31].

Someone like Ken could be trusted with another's property. If a person like Ken were to steal from another, their own minds would dole out shame and agony. Such an act is something that that person couldn't do without great regrets. It can also make them more aware of bad behavior in this area from others. It can prompt them to take actions against offenders that no one else would feel compelled to take.

The potential for conflict is high when two people with mismatched senses meet. The one is bound to offend the other into retaliatory action without even realizing it. This occurs in areas much less dramatic than theft, too. It can occur when two people have a mismatch in their sense of honesty, hard work, fair payment for fair work, and much more. Reciprocity can cause a hidden destruction of solidarity without the offender's even knowing why. It's this mechanism we'll discuss next.

The Hidden Destruction of Solidarity

Reciprocity's subconscious effects can be incredibly powerful, even if you're watching for them. To explain, let's look at a composite story from the workplace. Details have been changed to respect people's privacy.

In the past, I've been fortunate to work with some very talented people on several ongoing projects. These projects are protected by nondisclosure agreements, so please forgive some vagueness. Each project took a lot of hard work from many different people. However, once completed, each success brought satisfaction shared by those involved.

After completing several of these, I learned an unaffiliated coworker had been discussing our work with his higher-ups. He talked as if he were an authority over our projects. He also gave himself some credit for our accomplishments. For whatever reason, he felt no shame in this. I'd seen him do the same thing to others before. Taking unearned accolades didn't bother him.

What did matter to him was his reputation. He couldn't pass up an opportunity to enhance it. In terms of reciprocity, he seemed to have more anxiety over what happened to his reputation than over the telling of small lies.

However, honesty is something I care about. So is fair compensation for value added. Making sure others receive their fair due is something I go out of my way to ensure. Watching another flippantly take what wasn't earned felt particularly frustrating.

Between us we had a clear mismatch in our values. His actions had caused me offense that he wasn't even aware of. Even if I had explained it to him, I'm not sure he would have felt much shame.

However, I wanted to see what my own subconscious would do. Theoretically, the imbalance between us should lower my solidarity for him. My sense of reciprocity should nudge me to action against him. Since I was watching for this, I didn't know if either would happen. To my surprise, subconscious nudges came repeatedly and with surprising force.

The first nudge occurred when I was talking to his supervisor. She asked about his strengths, and I felt the sudden urge to downplay them. I resisted, and about a week later, his name came up in a hallway conversation with peers. I suddenly felt I should share my frustrations and warn them to protect their own work. Having withheld again, I found myself in a meeting several days later. He started bragging about things I knew he hadn't really done. My frustration flared again, and I strongly felt like calling him out in front of everyone.

I did say something in the meeting, although not with the force I felt was justified. Despite my earlier conscious decision to withhold action, I had taken a little anyway. It had just slipped through.

These impulses occurred against an otherwise good colleague, which was troubling enough. However, if I had spoken against him with full force at the meeting, it would have hurt him in the area he did care about: reputation. And while my sense of justice would have been satisfied, it would have also marked me as his enemy. Without understanding my reasons, my seemingly unwarranted attack would have lowered his solidarity for me. It would have made retaliatory actions against me more likely.

This could easily have started a self-propagating cycle of loss, further retaliation, and ever-lower solidarity. Each counterpunch would only have seemed to confirm that the other was a terrible person worthy of what they got. Both of us would have continuously made the other lose while the workplace around us became more toxic.

Meanwhile, our confused colleagues would wonder, "What's the matter with those two? They're otherwise good people. Why can't they see that in each other?"

There is a darker side to each principle in solidarity. For reciprocity, a mismatch between two people can cause one to deeply offend the other without realizing it. This can turn good people against each other without understanding why. By it, friendships fade, relationships sour, and coworkers turn into lifelong rivals.

We'll explore this further in chapter 4. Right now, there is one more mechanism by which solidarity is created and destroyed. And it's the darkest of this chapter.

The Dark Side of Trust and Respect

We've looked at the dark side of reciprocity. Now, let's see the same for trust and respect. "How in the world can trust and respect have a dark side?" We're about to find out.

Let's start small. What if I told you I have a small yellow "pill" that's about to become an international wonder cure? The substance is an energizer, and it might just hold keys to antiaging through spontaneous cell regeneration. Some are claiming it could lead to eternal youth.

You may be suspicious of this big claim, but let me assure you, we're always discovering new and wonderful things. Do you think we know all there is to know? Of course not! Do you think we've discovered all there is to discover? That'd be ridiculous!

The exact data on what this substance does are being tested, but when it comes to your health, why should you wait for that slow scientific process? There are all kinds of new treatments with this substance available now that are believed to be health promoting. There is one called the afternoon cure, where you sit in a card parlor enjoying time with friends while taking in the pill's warm glow. There is another treatment you eat with food. Another, you can simply drink. Sure, these can be expensive, but don't you think your health is worth it? Let's not fool ourselves. You are worth more than mere money!

They say the top scientists in the country are marveling at this new discovery. Why, even its discoverer, Dr. Curie, is going to win a Nobel Prize. With a name like Curie, you know it's going to be good medicine [32] [33].

OK, where are we? Well, it's 1901, and excitement is building around radium. It's an element that's six orders of magnitude (one million times) more radioactive than uranium [34]. And before the dangers of radioactivity were understood, a radium craze was making the rounds. Companies put it in food, drinks, and radium rooms to help the public better absorb "healthful" emissions.

Marketers freely used scientists' names and quotes. It didn't matter if they took words out of context or if facts had to be stretched. The public was desperate for better medicine, and companies were only too happy to sell it to them.

Why weren't people more skeptical? Why were they so eager to jump on the radiation bandwagon? It's because of the marketers' message.

People wanted to believe their health problems could be cured and age-related degeneration could be overcome. Marketers were there to tell people what they wanted to believe. They appeared to be on the public's side, helping them overcome the very unbelief the public desperately wanted to overcome. And when someone appears to be on your side, solidarity tends to rise. With it, respect and trust can follow.

However, the hype died as high doses of radiation did what high levels of radiation do. Even small doses can cause major harm. Some people's outcomes were tremendously horrific.

It's counterintuitive, but if radium were less immediately destructive, it would have had the chance to spread farther before its overwhelming harm ended the craze. The less immediately destructive an idea, and the more it promises, the further it can potentially spread. While it spreads, the idea's promotors enrich themselves through the sale of public poison and the glowing admiration of those who want their words to be true. This is one mechanism by which the promoters of bad ideas gain their followers trust and respect.

Let's see another, more telling example. Consider the superstition "rain follows the plow." Hundreds of years ago, there was a common superstition that the dry areas of Earth would remain dry until people tried growing crops. If people but tried to settle barren wastes, the land itself would know, and a rich bounty of rain would fall to sustain their efforts.

Imagine living in an overcrowded city where all good land is owned by others and opportunities for a better life are scarce. One day, a wanderer comes to town. He proclaims "rain follows the plow." Perhaps you've heard about it before and that it didn't work out for groups who tried. But this man claims he knows the "right" way. Where others have failed, he has seen success. He can lead you to a better life if you but sell your belongings to follow him. He promises a lifetime of full bellies and freedom from oppression.

The man's bold words ignite a fire in some listeners. Over time, the wanderer gathers a following of hopefuls who are dissatisfied with the status quo. These hopefuls house him. They feed him. They give him money to promote his important message. Meanwhile, their children listen to his words with wonder.

Followers want his words to be true, and his words help them believe what they want to believe. He's completely on their side in this, and when someone appears to be on your side, solidarity tends to rise. With it, trust and respect rise as well. The halo effect causes the rest of this man's unknown characteristics to seem increasingly positive. The man's faults in speech seem understandable. His factual missteps seem more forgivable. His wisdom seems more plentiful. In their minds, he transforms into a wise sage helping raise humanity to new heights.

But an outside observer sees no such transformation. Instead, they see a madman who is delusional at best and a pathological liar at worst. They find the ease at which he gathers followers unsettling. If this outsider tries to talk reason to the adamant followers, it's an uphill fight. By speaking against these followers' desires, the outsider appears to be working against them. When someone works against your goals, solidarity tends to drop, taking understanding and the willingness to listen along with it.

When their leader hears of outside opposition, he squirms and whines before accusing the outsider of trying to squelch his "truths" to keep the people in poverty and oppression. As much as possible, the leader cultivates an us-versus-them mentality. It raises his own followers' loyalty and binds them to him in common cause.

Many factors now work against the outsider. If solidarity drops, the outsider immediately seems less intelligent, less relatable, and less worthy of trust. If the outsider continues to argue, and solidarity continues to drop, then followers may lose all trust in the outsider and any other source of opposing facts. Their high solidarity for a beautiful lie makes them unreachable. Solidarity, trust, and respect have essentially trapped them in their own minds.

As soon as someone wants to believe in a thing, they'll eagerly throw in with whatever champion appears, even if that champion is completely unworthy of their trust, support, or respect. Followers trade all they own so they can plant good seed where it cannot grow. Entire groups of would-be communities lose their time, material possessions, and lives trusting the sage words of madmen.

When we tell people something they like or want to believe, solidarity tends to rise. When we tell them something they don't like, solidarity tends to fall. So, if we have to deliver bad news to the unreceptive, how can we do it? How can we reach the unreachable?

Chapter Four
Solidarity Rule Sets for Personal Life and Business

In this chapter, we'll see how solidarity can improve personal life and business relationships. We'll look at several circumstances where one person interacts directly with another. We'll also tie together what we've learned with greater detail.

Interaction Rules

All of us develop interaction rules throughout our lives. These make up the habits, tendencies, and attitudes we have toward different groups and situations. Some of these help us succeed. Others do not.

To better introduce this idea, consider the following story. My wife has been purchasing a product for years. However, the company that makes this product decided to "improve" it by changing its composition. In her opinion, it was a change for the worse. She wrote the company with her concerns, and someone there replied.

From a purely mechanical point of view, their reply had four main points:
- We've already "improved" this product.
- If you don't like it, learn to like it.
- We're not going to change anything.
- We want you to feel like you matter to us.

All four of these are selfish. If the company sent this list as written, it would have been insulting. However, they worded this list differently. Try spotting these selfish four points in the company's actual response: "Thank you for your concerns. We're always looking to improve our products, and this particular item has recently gone through our improvement process. We hope this new version will grow on you. We'll continue to look for feedback so we can provide the very best products for our customers."

Most companies have strong rules for how they deal with customers. They rarely deviate from these rules because they are hyperaware of what will happen if they do. In their response, the selfishness isn't apparent because someone's gone out of their way to reply to criticism graciously. This is part of their default rule set when interacting with other people.

What if they didn't? Let's look at Bob, a recently promoted head of a company's product improvement team. He's spent months of time, labor, testing, and money to make, at least in his opinion, one of their products better. He's worked with technicians and engineers to retool the factory and retrain the workforce. He's worked with the marketing department to redesign packaging extolling the product's new virtues. Finally, when the product becomes available, he begins working through customer feedback.

He's expecting the usual complaints that come in whenever there is change. However, after several months, complaints don't slow down. It gets to him, and his frustration builds. Finally, a customer writes him with a particularly detailed set of concerns. She urges him to revert to the previous, more beloved version of the product. But Bob has had it. He replies: "You are just one person in billions. We can't cater to everyone's whims. Do you know how much time, effort, and money went into this change? Just how egocentric are you to demand we go back because you don't like it? Only an idiot would miss how much better we've made this product for you. Now you have 'concerns'? Forget it!"

What happens? In our increasingly connected age, Bob's angry rant is shared and shared again. It's shared from the point of view of a consumer being badgered by a large company for offering honest feedback. The more the response is shared, the more the company is seen as uncaring. The company's value drops, and its leaders realize they have to do something. They fire their recently promoted head of product improvement. They make public apologies. They promise to do better in the future. These are the consequences of one person's words.

So responses like Bob's are rare. When dealing with consumers, companies tend to be on the consumers' side as much as possible, show them respect, and thank them for their feedback.

And yet, in our own lives, many people don't understand that their tone, appearance, and word choice will have future consequences for them personally. Let's look at a more telling example.

Rule Sets That Will Destroy Marriages

The following phenomenon is sometimes called Walk-Away Spouse Syndrome. It's the name given when one spouse, in a way that can appear sudden and without warning, leaves a relationship. It's something solidarity can help explain.

Derk and Amanda married "for time and eternity" in their church. They were a strong, beautiful couple as committed to each other as to the ideals of a successful marriage. Derk was intelligent, socially savvy, and hardworking. Amanda was compassionate, introspective, and, at times, hilarious. They had the makings of a power couple in their social circle.

Several years and some children later, Derk worked full time while finishing a degree in business. Amanda worked from home, helping put Derk through school while raising their young children. Both she and her husband were religious and had important volunteer positions in their house of worship. From the outside, all seemed well.

But their homelife told a different story. Each night, Derk returned to find their house a mess, with energetic young ones running wild and a weary wife. Their conversations centered on daily complaints, problems, and lists of things Amanda needed Derk to do around the house. Returning home became Derk's least favorite part of day.

Amanda, meanwhile, was exhausted. Their youngest was two years old and still woke her up screaming each night. Her other children acted out because they wanted more attention than Amanda could give. Moreover, Amanda sometimes felt like a single mom—one that had to care for an additional man-child who required constant pushing to do his daily chores.

Amanda knew of the distance in her relationship. She knew her marriage needed attention. But what time was there? With jobs, Derk's schooling, their children, and their willing obligations to their community, other things just seemed more important.

But maybe things were improving? Derk used to complain loudly when she asked for help, but that had stopped. Maybe he had started to understand what she needed?

But from Derk's perspective, they didn't talk or enjoy each other's time, and their interactions caused complaining and guilt. He tried fighting back, but nothing improved. Eventually, he realized, "I'm not sure what love is, but I know I don't feel it for her." He gave up, merely going through the motions at home. He'd looked for emotional connection elsewhere and had found it in one of his coworkers. The coworker reciprocated, too.

Derk returned one day with an announcement. "I'm done. I'm not doing this anymore. I want you and the kids out." I don't know the rest of their conversation, but a moving van appeared outside their apartment the next day. Then there was no more Amanda.

Derk and Amanda don't share equal blame. What they did share was a similar attitude toward the other: "other things are more important right now." Let's look at this failed marriage again through the lens of what we've learned in this book.

When they first married, the excitement and newness of their relationship had made each day feel like an adventure. Their days had been filled with enjoying each other's company and conversing about their future plans. Interactions had been highly positive. Both had felt in love, and it had brought them closer together as solidarity had risen higher.

As their infatuation for each other had worn away, so had some enthusiasm. Derk, feeling a little disenchanted with his marriage, had put more attention into his career. Amanda, sensing Derk's change of focus, had put her attention into their first pregnancy, which had started with terrible morning sickness. Their conversations had become less frequent and centered on the stresses of work and the strains of pregnancy. As time had continued, talking about complaints had become normal. It had made time pass, but it hadn't been enjoyable. Derk had even found himself avoiding Amanda.

Derk and Amanda had used to work household chores together without keeping track of who had done what and for how long. However, as Derk had lost interest in their relationship, Amanda had found herself doing more on her own. Slowly, she had begun to feel that Derk wasn't on her side on the home front. It had caused her solidarity for him to erode a little more. At first, she had politely said, "I've done the dishes the last three days. Would you mind doing them tonight?" It had become, "Would you actually lift a finger to help around here?" As Derk had seen it, her "nagging" was causing him to draw further away, and their solidarity had dropped a little more.

Physical intimacy has been shown to raise solidarity by flooding the brain with "oxytocin and vasopressin," which are "linked with the attachment system in the brain" [35]. Intimacy can be a binding force between two people, helping to raise solidarity between them. It's one of the forces that keep two people completely wrong for each other from moving on.

Before Derk and Amanda's schism, physical intimacy had been something they enjoyed. It had been enough to counteract most of their negative interactions. With it, their relationship had held together with a midlevel of solidarity. At that stage, things hadn't been great, but they hadn't been falling apart yet either.

However, more children and stress had changed that. As we saw in chapter 2, stress tends to lower solidarity for those around us. Both had started snapping at the other for things that normally wouldn't matter. Amanda had come to see Derk less like a man juggling too many responsibilities and more like a source of mess and irritation. Derk had come to see Amanda less like a life partner in need of help and more like an incessant complainer. When he had started avoiding her entirely, their physical intimacy had dried up.

When there is little raising solidarity and too much dragging it down, a relationship deteriorates. In this case, it had deteriorated faster for Derk than it had for Amanda. When one of Derk's coworkers had offered emotional connection, Derk hadn't resisted as he otherwise might have. The rest is this couple's sad history.

We all can get so much about dating and marriage wrong, and when we do, it can drag us through the depths of human misery. So what if a couple hits extremely low periods, both asking themselves if their marriage was a mistake? What if a couple has personal limitations that work to wedge them apart? What if both reach the point where divorce is brought up constantly in their conversations? Is that it for them?

Years ago, just these last questions could have summarized my own marriage. Many times it seemed it could all go wrong. And yet, to my great happiness, it didn't. Since there was no abuse or infidelity, and since we could be great friends, we knew we were living far below our own potential. So we made a few small changes.

First, we became more aware of the effects of our words and actions on each other. We tried making our conversations more fun by focusing not just on problems but also on what we both enjoyed. Each time concerns came up that seemed more important than each other, we reinvested in our friendship instead. All three of these increased our solidarity for each other. And despite both our flaws, we were able to reach new heights I didn't think were reachable. It replaced our disillusionment and frustration with excitement for the next day in our journey together.

Solidarity gives us tools, and awareness gives us choices. When we make building solidarity our default rule set, it changes the way our brains perceive another. It turns the imperfect mundane into the imperfect exceptional.

Let's look at solidarity-building rules that can help improve our personal and professional lives in more detail.

Rule Set: Value Awareness

A fellow engineer related this story. Her department had decided to save costs by eliminating janitorial services. She was responsible for equipment valued in the millions and now needed to empty out the office's paper waste—take out the trash, replace the bag, and repeat as needed. Although irritating and perhaps a questionable use of her time, she didn't think it was a huge deal. At least until the department manager visited.

"No," the manager told her. "You're putting the bag in wrong."

"Does it matter?" she asked.

"It's not how we do things here." The manager gathered the entire department together for an impromptu training exercise. He taught them how to "properly" put a bag in the trash can. Over the next weeks, if a bag wasn't replaced "properly," the manager would interrupt her and the other engineers until someone fixed it. While they fixed it, he would offer his free advice on how to do it better.

As a reader, and knowing nothing else, do you have an impression of this manager? Is this someone you'd go out of your way to do favors for? If this manager were demoted for wasting another's time, would you feel a little satisfaction? I know my answers to these questions.

This is an example of lacking awareness of our actions. While the manager felt powerful and important, their actions said that everyone else lacked the basic intelligence to be trusted with simple tasks. This is a form of continuous disrespect that lowers solidarity.

Some people are extra sensitive to this. They see it as a form of oppression and bullying. They cannot function at peak performance in such an environment.

Let's see this from another perspective. While working in Alaska, we had a particularly detail-oriented captain. The captain was responsible for the safety of everyone on the ship, so normally this would be an excellent trait. However, without realizing it, his extreme sensitivity to safety created more problems than it solved.

One of his biggest triggers was seeing a kink form in any hose, no matter its importance. So let's say you were spraying down the deck with a garden hose, and it briefly kinked. If he saw you, and he was always watching for bad behavior, then you brought down his wrath. The helm's side window would slide open, and there would be a shower of profanity loud enough to echo across the bay. Then it would go quiet as the captain disappeared from view. Moments later, he'd emerge on deck. With arms flailing like windmills, he'd follow the offending crew member around, talking about everything that was being done wrong. Then, breathing heavily, the captain would puff his way back to the helm to continue his vigil until he spotted the next offense.

Of course, the structural integrity of a flexible fluid transport system (i.e., hose) is important. However, obsessions like these made the crew hate him.

For amusement, they started going out of their way to muss up his orderly systems. They responded to his priorities slowly. When he pressed them, they found endless excuses for why basic tasks took so long. These small acts of retribution delighted the crew. Meanwhile, other projects stalled as crew members redirected their attention to things without real worth.

These last two examples are from the workplace, but they readily translate to home. Do we constantly nag our significant other about the proper way to take out the trash, load the dishwasher, or make the bed? Or do our actions make the other feel important, appreciated, and valued? Do we belittle others and their imperfections? Or do we celebrate their imperfect efforts on our behalf?

If we don't understand the effect of our words and actions on others, we destroy another's solidarity for us without realizing it. We gain another's resistance to our goals, pleasure at our struggles, and unwillingness to take our ideas seriously. Conversely, when we build awareness, we gain control over the consequences of our words and actions. Through these, we gain control over our own futures.

Rule Set: Be on Their Side

"So that's why I didn't turn in the exam." The student looked at me expectantly. "Can I please have one more extension?"

The student had missed the deadline for a take-home exam by a week. He had reasons for missing it. But I had already made the solutions public. I also knew other students had struggled to make the deadline while juggling their own personal difficulties and obligations. How would accepting late work be fair to them? For both reasons, I knew I shouldn't accept the late exam.

Other professors get frustrated when students make this request. They tell them "no" and to "suck it up" and that they "need to learn personal responsibility." Years ago, and based on these examples, I clumsily handled my own situations like this. It ended with a couple students openly despising me.

So what do I really value here? Showing compassion? Asserting authority? Helping a student learn personal responsibility? Avoiding conflict so we can all get along better in the future? Being on the student's side?

At first, these may seem mutually incompatible. However, solidarity gives us paths that can achieve all simultaneously.

Instead of lecturing, I responded with understanding. "I get where you're coming from. Sometimes life dumps on us. I understand that better than most. I've talked with other professors about situations like this one. It's their policy to never give extensions once solutions are out. With that said, let's see if we can find your best options."

He nodded, so I used the time I might have spent lecturing in a different way.

We looked at the grade book. "You could still pass if you turned in the rest of the homework and aced the final. However, that's going to require a lot of time, and it sounds like you don't have much with everything else going on right now." This was true. He was struggling to keep up in his other classes, and he was battling sizable challenges at home.

"You could also drop the course without affecting your GPA. That would give you time to focus on your other courses and probably relieve stress considerably. I'll, of course, be offering this again next spring." Again, my focus was on the parts of this choice that would benefit him most.

"Finally, we might be able to get you into a streaming version of this course this summer. It's accelerated, but since you've already worked through some of it, it should be easier the second time. This will also keep your graduation date on track."

After a short discussion, he decided to take the second option. He gratefully thanked me for my understanding and time. From a purely mechanical point of view,

- authority was asserted;
- personal responsibility came through natural consequences;
- there was no criticism;

- helping another find the best options dissolved conflict; and
- solidarity was built since I had been on his side every step of the way.

What if I had lectured? Like some professors, I might have said, "Look, this is the real world. You need to start taking your life seriously. Everyone else took care of their personal problems without seeking bailout. You shouldn't even be in my office asking for one. You'll have to take the grade you get, and there is nothing you can do about it."

If my default response were to embarrass and shame, I'd be followed by low solidarity's negative effects. I'd signal, "I may be your professor, but don't bring me your problems." Far fewer, if any, students would come to my office for help, and that would hamstring my ability to teach complex material. Lower solidarity would siphon enjoyment from my classes. Offended students would be less willing to go along with my nightly dumb jokes that already need as much help as they can get. And since the program I teach for depends on word of mouth, negative reviews would drive away new students.

All other factors being equal, one rule set change would make me less proficient at my entire job.

There are so many different situations where conflict should be inevitable. Sometimes we're dealing with a difficult personality determined to cause us problems. Sometimes we're asking for help from higher-ups already swamped with other concerns. Sometimes we're trying to make new friends in hostile environments.

But when we actively try to be on another's side, we construct a web of new connections and community. We gain people we can count on, just as they gain us. We become surrounded by those willing to understand and support our goals.

It takes practice. It takes awareness. It might not work out every time. But when it does, everyone's life is enriched. The takeaway is simple: be on another's side as much as you can in the areas you can support.

Rule Set: Work with Reciprocity

Let's go deeper. In chapter 3, we learned how the reciprocity effect prompts actions, tracks favors and offenses, and creates social guardians in the areas that are most important to them. Through reciprocity, we find the hidden creation and destruction of solidarity. Does someone trample over the things that matter to you? They may be unaware of the offense. Meanwhile, we cannot fathom how someone would miss something so obvious. How can we use this?

First, it changes how we build solidarity for another. We cannot be "on their side" through the things they don't care about. The best way to see this is through an example.

Jim is a recent graduate hired to work for a small business in his city. He's built up his résumé through several temp positions, and he's looking forward to a permanent position. He's been told his professionalism, efficiency, and reliability are top-notch. At his last position, he earned the temp-of-the-year award. Jim feels great about this. He's excited to see where his hard work will take him.

Sue owns the small business that's hired him. Like Jim, Sue works hard at what she does. For her business, she puts great effort into making her clients feel welcome and cared for. If a client calls with late-in-the-day problems, Sue stays late to solve them, even if she has to cancel personal plans. It's not something she really thinks about. Rather, it's part of who she is. Because of her commitment to her profession and her clients, Sue's business has grown to the point that she's overwhelmed. Hence, why she's hired Jim.

She chose Jim over several promising applicants because Jim was so highly recommended by his past employers. Also, his résumé and cover letter were the most organized. By the halo effect, Jim's positive reputation and applicant materials have made him seem better in all of his unknown areas, including his interpersonal skills and understanding of the service industry. So Sue's confidence in Jim starts high.

However, this changes during Jim's first week. When Jim meets with clients, he doesn't take the time to know them. He doesn't go out of his way to make them feel welcome. Instead, he acts more like a machine grinding through one client's problem to get to the next. He's completely impersonal with them, too. With this one hire, the whole feel of her business has changed.

What is wrong with him? If they don't go out of their way to take care of clients, they'll lose them. Only an idiot would miss something so obvious. Sue tries communicating her disapproval through the looks she gives him and the comments she makes: "Whoa, slow down there, buddy. This isn't a race" and "Maybe you should try getting to know each client. You know, be friendlier." Jim nods each time, but it doesn't seem to change much. Sue's not sure he's getting it. Maybe he'll settle in more next week?

Jim, meanwhile, feels he's had a good start. For him, taking care of clients means respecting their time. So he's worked hard to get their problems solved quickly. There were a lot of clients, but he got through his list with time to spare. He watched Sue, on the other hand, chat up each of hers. Even though she worked with the complex cases while Jim handled the simple ones, each seemed to take Sue far longer than it should have. Maybe Sue didn't value hard work? That would be unfortunate. He'd find that hard to respect.

The other thing bothering Jim is Sue's looks of disapproval. He wonders what he's doing wrong. Maybe he isn't working hard enough? He resolves to work even faster in the future.

So Jim aims to build solidarity with his boss through the areas he cares about. He wants to impress her. He wants her approval. He sees fast, efficient work as a reliable way to show he's on her side. But Sue sees things differently. Even though both value hard work, they value it in different ways. This mismatch in reciprocity has already lowered solidarity for each other. Sue thinks Jim may be unable to listen or care. Jim thinks

Sue doesn't value hard work. And when solidarity lowers, it makes understanding between two people even harder.

Sue watches Jim spend even less time with clients. Her frustration builds. Is this guy stupid or just completely ineffectual? How could anyone recommend him for anything? During their first break, she's more direct with him. "Slow down," she tells him. "You're going way too fast." But Jim doesn't understand what she's really saying. So Jim replies, "Why don't you try speeding up? You might get more done."

At the end of week two, she schedules a performance review. Sue's values, goals, and sensitivities have made Jim appear cold and mechanical. It's what she now sees as his most defining traits, and this makes the halo effect work against him. She gives him low scores in many other areas, too.

Jim leaves hurt and angry. What kind of insensitive monster is she? Solidarity lowers further, and their interactions become increasingly negative. By month's end, Sue fires Jim. When she does, strong words are exchanged. Some clients overhear and never return to Sue's business.

Both of these hardworking individuals were blind to the other. Both were left worse because of it. And yet their unique values would have otherwise complimented each other. Jim's hard work would have quickly and efficiently knocked out the busy work of two regular employees. Sue's sensitivity to her clients would mean continuous growth for her business. But as solidarity lowered between them, both found it harder to see the positive qualities in the other.

No matter how hard Jim worked, it was against Sue's sense of reciprocity. While trying to be on her side, he unknowingly trampled over the things Sue cared about most. To actually be on her side, he needed to work *with* her sense of reciprocity by making her clients feel valued, important, and cared for. However, Jim wasn't aware she valued these things, so he never had this choice.

There are so many different values, goals, and senses of reciprocity: hard work, honesty, supporting each other no matter what, getting things done, ensuring fairness, being reliable, connecting through conversation, having fun together, understanding the other, working toward a goal, and so many more.

When we try to support someone outside of areas they care about, we can cause offense, make them feel disrespected, and make ourselves unrelatable. They don't see the value we try to add, and we don't understand how they miss it. If, instead, we support people in areas they care about, we effectively speak their language. They feel we understand them, share their values, and are on their side on a deeper level. Solidarity is then free to rise as they are better able to see our positive qualities.

Is there a way to know what other people's sensitivities are? Is there a way to know our own?

Rule Set: Observe Actions

If you want to know someone's goals, values, and sensitivities, including your own, observe actions. What do we actually put effort into? Is this effort consistent, or does it fluctuate over time? The more consistent the action, the potentially stronger the cognitive force behind it.

For example, if you wanted to build solidarity with Sue as an employee, she feels you're on her side when you support her clients. We know this because it's what she herself works so hard to accomplish. It's such a part of her that she feels this strength should be obvious to everyone. And yet her business grows where others' do not because of what she thinks "should be obvious to everyone." It speaks directly to Sue's unique talent, potential for success, and true self.

What about Jim? Jim shows up, gets things done, and tries to make his employer happy. When someone acknowledges these things, Jim feels appreciated and respected. When someone works hard, Jim feels he understands them on a deep level. When he sees Sue "wasting" time with small talk, he balks. Until he sees that Sue's small talk is a form of hard work, he'll never understand or completely respect his boss. If someone helped him see this connection, things could be different.

We can know a person's values, goals, and sense of reciprocity by watching their actions. Their words can help, but there is danger in relying on words alone. For example, any liar can say they are honest. How do you know the difference between a habitual liar and someone who is truly honest? Truly honest people will take responsibility for mistakes, even at personal cost. If they didn't, they wouldn't feel right about themselves. Their personal sense of reciprocity won't allow that without haunting them with deep shame. For them, they'll respect the true and take greater offense at the false and pretentious.

Does someone value hard work, or do they just like appearing like a hard worker? After all, any freeloader benefits when they can blend in. How can you tell the difference? People who really value hard work will consistently work hard. If they didn't, they couldn't look at themselves in the mirror the same way.

Does someone value loyalty, or do they only value what it gets them? After all, the most treacherous can insist on the most personal allegiance. Having loyal followers helps protect people from the consequences of their own deceits. How can you tell the difference? Truly loyal people will go out of their way to support their friends when there is trouble, even when it's not convenient or when it requires sacrifice. For them, there is no other way to live. They'll be more likely to notice betrayals, even small ones, and react more strongly against those individuals.

To summarize, the more a person really values something, the more distress they feel acting against it. They will be more likely to notice bad behavior in others and reject offenders, even if the offenders have no idea what they're doing wrong. When solidarity lowers over these mismatches, it blinds people to another's true worth, increasing conflict and misunderstanding.

But by learning people's core values, we learn something fundamental about who they are. It shows us the lines they refuse to cross and the actions they can only perform with great personal difficulty. It also shows us the ways we can best support them in their lives. It allows us to connect with them on a deeper level.

This rule set alone has improved many aspects of my own life.

It has changed the way I speak in front of an audience. If my message is made up of only a couple notes, I will only reach a small part of my audience with it. The rest of the audience who care about other things will end up uninterested and unengaged, at least until I've connected my message to something they do care about.

So, for example, if I'm lecturing to a group of working adults in a night class, I know they're coming in tired, distracted, and possibly hungry. Having snacks at the door helps the hungriest focus. Presenting with interesting visuals helps the most tired stay awake. Having a few dumb jokes can be appreciated by the most stressed. Reminding the audience why the message can help them personally gives them better reason to care. The more of these I include, the more of my audience I can reach, and the less boring my late-night lectures become.

It has changed the way I give tours. By chatting with a group before a tour, I learn some things that matter to them. Then, in the tour, I can emphasize those points, which increases engagement, interest, and overall experience.

For example, I was giving a tour to an accreditation agency. I learned one evaluator had a strong sense of self-reliance, believing that a person should sink or swim by their own effort. Another evaluator valued results over a strict adherence to rules. To appeal to both, I told the one, "This is our machine shop. We're setting up a sign-in system. That way, if a student leaves even a small mess, we can fail them." The first evaluator nodded approvingly. I turned to the other evaluator and said, smiling, "We won't really fail them." The second evaluator nodded approvingly. Having several moments like this helped the tour go far better than it otherwise could have.

It has changed the way I relate to others. No one wants a person to dominate conversation with the things they alone have been obsessively working on and thinking about. Rather, others want to talk about the things that matter to them with another who values the importance of what they say. Learning what matters to other people, and discovering for myself why it's important, has expanded my otherwise limited talent for small talk. This has allowed me to forge friendships with those who were previously inaccessible.

Observe actions. When we see what people put effort into, we learn more about their potential, strengths, and how to best reach with them.

Rule Set: Reject Habitual Liars

Sometimes the most obvious rules are the least used because familiarity can blind. I learned of a "friend" who was lying to me repeatedly. I didn't want to believe it was true, but once I finally became more aware, I found the lies to be casual, habitual, and for their benefit at my personal cost. It took far longer to realize the betrayal than I'm comfortable admitting. My solidarity with them was just too high, and many lies were things I wanted to believe.

If someone asks, "If someone lies to you repeatedly, can you still believe them?" I understand how the answer can be yes, at least for a time. Liars know this, too. They know they can bind us to themselves by manipulating our values, desires, and sense of outrage. And if our solidarity for them is high, it's hard for those with better information to reach us.

But a lack of skepticism can cause serious harm to ourselves and society.

When radium was being touted as a health cure, it slowly destroyed its users. Those who used it the longest experienced the greatest harms. Who benefited from this deception? The companies stretching the truth so they could sell more poison. When our foreparents followed "rain follows the plow" and planted seed where insufficient rain would ever fall, they lost their time, resources, and lives. The most stubborn suffered the longest. Meanwhile, leaders bathed in their admiration and could freely abuse their positions of power. Throughout history, this trend has continued until enough people realize the deception and end the betrayal.

There is really no way around it. The degree we entertain liars in our own lives is the degree we risk our own decline for their enrichment.

This has never been more important to understand. We live in an interconnected world. This brings us ever closer to both the best and worst among us. The best will occasionally make mistakes and own them. The worst will hide their mistakes while shaming the honest for admitting their faults.

This is a solidarity insanity, not unlike the ones we'll discuss in chapter 5. When a society hyperfocuses on another's small missteps, it encourages more people to lie about their own. Punishing the small can make the whole of society worse. Meanwhile, the dishonest continue to mislead the rest of us in punishing the honest for their honesty.

We can find habitual liars nearly anywhere. While there may not be many of them, their potential for harm is far greater than their numbers. We can find them in politicians, news anchors, and public personalities. These individuals thrive by manipulating our fears, angers, and outrages. They enrich themselves while the rest of society is left in delusion and loss.

The more we realize that habitual lies are a form of deep betrayal, and the more we reject these acts, the more protection we gain from these harms. This rule set isn't just about protecting ourselves. It helps protect everyone else, too. The more we choose to speak against habitual acts of corruption, exaggeration, and lies, the better we watch out for everyone in society. If enough people rejected habitual liars, even the beautiful ones we adore, the greater all our lives could be enriched.

Rule Set: Rejoice in Honest Struggle

There is an important question we haven't asked. Are values, goals, and senses of reciprocity fixed? This is an extremely important question. If they are fixed, we have no way to really understand others different from us. We have no way to develop ourselves in new areas.

But I believe this question has a definitive answer.

As a child, I didn't realize how valuable reliable facts, self-awareness, and hard work would be to me. But part of growing as an individual is discovering the value the previously unknown can add to one's own life. I learned the value of hard work on ships in Alaska from peers I respected. Hard work could make one valuable to an organization and provide better financial security and control over the future. Reliable facts through education deepened my respect for what we become through what we continuously learn. Self-honesty became important as my youthful delusions clashed with my desire to understand how the real world worked.

If I thought each of my values were fixed throughout time, then I'd never expect to be much different at age thirty-seven from age twenty-seven from age seventeen from age seven. Yet each decade brought significant change. If I didn't think I could ever change, I would deny my own capacity to grow as a person.

When it comes to personal growth, I'm not alone. We are all capable of discovering and developing new, previously unknown values that greatly enrich our own lives. Perhaps we shouldn't give up on ourselves, or others, just because there is some area perceived as weak. If we dismiss others, or ourselves, too soon, we deny a truth of existence: all of us can become more than we currently are.

And for someone to do anything new, interesting, or valuable, there will be struggle and missteps. Without a clear road, there will be greater imperfection. But the more we punish ourselves and others for small imperfections, the less we all try. If we are to reach our highest potential, perhaps we shouldn't just tolerate honest struggle—we should rejoice in it.

But all this brings us to a different set of questions that, if thought about seriously, may be the most uncomfortable in this book:

- Do our conflated indignations blind us to other people's developing talents?
- Are we all too quick to punish one another over our misunderstandings and missteps?
- Has low solidarity caused us to despise those who are strong in an area we are not?

I don't know the answers, but consider the stories from just this chapter. When good people like Jim and Sue and Amanda and Derk implode for completely avoidable reasons, it adds to the total sum of human misery on this earth. How much suffering could we thwart if enough people were just a little more aware of one another's true potentials?

Chapter Five
Solidarity and the World

The solidarity effect is everywhere. While I was finishing up this book, my family took a trip to the mountains. We stopped for lunch, and our server took an instant liking to us. He first gave us free drinks. Then, when his manager wasn't looking, he gave us coupons for free items. When I offered to just pay for them, he stopped me. "Just take them. This company doesn't care about me. Why should I care about it?"

We continued our journey, discussing one of my friend's troubles. He was new to his position, having just completed six long, expensive years in medical school. Weeks before, he had offended one of his coworkers with some of his louder opinions. The coworker had combed through my friend's online presence and found more opinions they found offensive. Outraged, the coworker had cherry-picked quotes, compiled a list, and shared the list with their entire office. The coworker had then lodged a formal complaint declaring my friend unsuitable for his job. Seemingly overnight, his entire department had turned on him, and he had been left explaining how his words were taken out of context and apologizing for offenses he hadn't meant.

When we arrived at our lodgings, the outer property was littered with construction debris. The construction should have been finished weeks ago, but there was an ongoing dispute between contractors over who was in charge of what. The day before, one contractor had gotten into a screaming match with another, and the owner had kicked them both off the premises.

Finally, near sunset, I listened to the troubles of one of my wife's relations. They had recently bought their first house, but unbeknownst to them, the back of it was part of an incomplete public trail. The city was working to renovate this trail and put public access through their driveway. This would mean strangers walking through their yard at all hours of the day, something neither of them felt comfortable with, especially since they had young children. The couple reacted to the city with aggressive fury. The issue turned into a power struggle between them and the city council. Unfortunately, it's this council that ultimately decides their property's fate.

Solidarity's consequences are real, ongoing, and greatly affect an individual's, society's, or nation's overall success and failure. When neighbors don't like one another, spite replaces cooperation. When employees feel like their employer is against them, they actively work against their employer's goals. Zooming out, when leaders of countries can't get along, it's the people who pay through economic and social instability.

Our lack of awareness can cost all of us in ways both big and small. So let's take a big picture view of solidarity with applications for the workplace, society, and the world. Some systems we build only promote failure rather than success, and they don't have to. They are what I like to call solidarity insanities.

When We Make Cooperation Too Costly

The following allegory is a split hair away from the real world. It's more involved than I like, but I believe its potential depth is worth the relatively small investment in time. It also shows how complete insanity can come from a logical progression when we ignore solidarity's lessons.

Imagine you're working for an employee-owned manufacturing company. Your products have done well, but there is room for improvement in their reliability, durability, and affordability. Moreover, similar companies are now producing similar products. If your company is to survive, it needs to update its offerings.

This should be relatively simple. Your products have been on the market for some time, and there is lots of customer feedback. You know what parts usually fail. You have reviews stating what customers would like to see changed.

Some of these changes are common sense. Making them should improve products in ways both big and small. For example, assembly could be simplified to reduce manufacturing cost. A little reinforcement in places would prevent many of the reported failures. A small change to a product's form would increase ease of use. All you need are the engineers to work out the exact details.

However, little has come out of the engineering department in some time. What has been released has arguably made products worse, and sales have fallen. You approach one of the engineers to ask why. Why haven't they made even the common sense changes?

"You want products to be more reliable, functional, and more affordable?" the engineer asks doubtfully. "So you want more of everything?"

"Yes." You reply. "That would be nice." After all, the history of innovation and engineering is one of different groups working together to have more of everything possible. For example, take the advancement of computers. In the 1960s, computers were expensive, slow, room-sized energy-hungry monstrosities. But by the 1980s, computers had become vastly faster, smaller, cheaper, lighter, and more reliable. But even the best computers of the 1980s are put to shame by the most cost-effective ones of today. To really appreciate how far they've come, a room-sized 1960s computer took twenty-four hours to estimate coarse weather patterns one day in advance. In the 2000s, the same calculations could be run in less than a second on a single cheap handheld cell phone. Every decade, cost, weight, and power requirements have plummeted while speed, reliability, and functionality have skyrocketed. The innovators and engineers didn't just improve one aspect of their designs. They found ways to have more of everything.

Was this easy to do? Absolutely not. It required different people systematically working together to find better ways. They didn't always know how, and failures occurred, but so did successes. Each success meant a possible improvement to people's lives.

The accumulation of success created the modern age. Advancements continue each time someone asks, "I want more of everything; how can I get it?"

When you explain this to your engineer, he rubs at one eye. "You want it all? Even knowing how, you can't improve any aspect of our designs without making something worse."

"What do you mean?"

"Our engineering is zero-sum. If you want a product more durable, then it will also become less reliable. Or heavier. Or more expensive."

"That makes no sense," you reply. "What if we made a small change to a product's grip, making it easier to hold. How would that make something else worse?"

The engineer hesitates. "Truthfully? Our department might purposefully weaken a joint so the product was less reliable. Or they might make the assembly more complex to increase manufacturing cost. Or they might add weight to make the product harder to carry. We treat values as zero-sum. If something is made better, then we'll also make something worse by the same amount, if not more."

"That's absolutely ridiculous," you reply. "This sounds completely made up. Who would agree to something so idiotic?"

The engineer sighs. "We all did, although not explicitly. I wish I was making this up. Our zero-sum design rules started completely on their own. Every step leading to it was logical. In retrospect, possibly inevitable."

To your skeptical look, the engineer continues. "I'll try to explain the best I can…"

When the company started, the engineering department was divided in how it thought things should be run. There were two competing visions. One group wanted reliability to be the guiding value. After all, if a product failed at the wrong time, what use was it? And, once something had been proven to work, why change it?

The other group wanted products to be more functional, even if that meant scrapping previous, well-tested designs. Sure, this could create new problems, but if a new version could be made better, then the company would be successful. Everyone would benefit.

These points of view conflicted. Regular employees didn't know who to put in charge. So they invented a system. The two opposing groups would take turns being in a lead role. The lead role would have the majority of decision-making power. The other group would work in a support role with the remaining decision power. Every four weeks, the department's progress would be evaluated by employees. Then the two groups would switch roles.

If employees believed progress was good, the lead group would be rewarded with a tiny bit more decision-making power in the future. For the other group to regain it, it would also have to make progress as lead role when its turn came. This way, there would be friendly competition between groups to outperform each other.

Also, if a group really had better design values, then it would succeed more often as lead. Over time, this group would gain more of the decision-making power, causing better decisions to be made. This should allow the entire company to reach new heights over the long term.

Does this sound like a good system to you? It seems to cover many of the motivating parts of human nature. Challenge. Accomplishment. Competition.

But let's see what happened.

At the beginning, the two groups needed to get things done. They didn't have much choice. If the company was to survive, it had to create greatness together. Sure, there were loud disagreements, but the two groups always found a way forward. Failure was the leviathan that kept them in check. If they didn't solve problems and make better products, the entire company would go bankrupt. So as they worked through new prototypes, they made sure each version had more of everything possible.

But when successes made the company more stable, things began to change. Both groups had time to ask themselves what the company's future should really look like. Each group didn't trust where the other might lead the company if it had its own way. No one wanted the other to ruin what they all had worked so hard to create. Each group drew into itself, recommitting to its own values and strengthening its own internal ties.

Normally, strong group loyalty is thought of as positive. However, like much in solidarity, there is a far darker side, too.

One group realized a self-evident truth. Each time they did their job well as support, they lost influence. Cooperation was costing them. Cooperation hurt their own goals. And if their opponents succeeded too often, their opponent would gain more influence. Over time, this could cause their opponent's questionable values to ruin everything for everyone.

So, one team stopped working as hard each time they were in the support role. The other team found it harder to succeed as lead. Over several cycles, the status quo began shifting toward the ones who had stopped helping.

The betrayed group realized what was happening. If they really cared about the company, they needed their own values to be represented instead of trampled. If they wanted to preserve their values, they also needed to stop doing their job as support.

Progress slowed considerably. Since both groups were working against the other's goals, solidarity began to drop. The next cycles brought increased toxicity, decreased mutual support, and deepening challenges with understanding, empathy, and basic civility.

When solidarity fell far enough, a more troubling pattern emerged. Feeling hurt, angry, and betrayed, one group used their support role not just to slack but to sabotage. It started small. When one lead group tried reshaping a product's grip for increased durability and comfort, the support group added a few small sharp edges to make it painful to hold. At the end of the cycle, durability increased while comfort decreased. Ultimately, the design was worse. The next cycle, the lead group simplified assembly and removed most sharp edges that they had previously added. In response, the betrayed group preserved the worse of the sharp edges and added a slight bend to the handle, making it harder to hold. So affordability increased, but functionality decreased. The next cycle, the handle was mostly straightened, restoring functionality, but pinholes were added at key locations that decreased reliability.

Over many cycles, designs became stranger. Each betrayal caused the groups to blame the other. Other employees began to take sides. Some vowed to approve any design of their favored group, no matter how badly it performed, just to break the deadlock. This led to some of the stranger designs being put into production.

As the problem grew, more employees joined in. Some wanted to fire all the engineers. Some wanted to join the engineering department to sort out the mess themselves. The rest had so many problems of their own, they didn't have time for more. What they did want was for the engineering department to do their job before the entire company went bankrupt.

The engineer concludes the story: "This is why our marketing department has had to grow. It needs more people to sell increasingly inferior products. This is why customer service has doubled. Product returns have skyrocketed."

There is anger in the engineer's words. "This isn't a descent into insanity. It's arrival."

Solidarity Insanities

Solidarity insanities are deeply ironic, pitching what we expect against what we actually get. They occur when

- we make cooperation costlier than conflict;
- we mistake acts of betrayal for acts of group loyalty;
- we support those who propagate conflict instead of cooperation; and
- we create systems without stabilizing leviathans that punish needless conflict.

Let's explore these points further.

First, when we play zero-sum games that don't need to be zero-sum, we often set ourselves up for failure. Let's look at a few examples.

Let's say a company wants to increase production from employees. The company enacts a system that automatically fires the lowest performers each year. For employees near this margin, what happens? First, reasons to cooperate with one another vanish. The more each low performer helps another succeed, the greater the chance they'll lose their own job. Because employees are competing against one another, they work against one another's goals. This lowers cooperation, understanding, and civility.

Is this limited only to bottom performers? An increase of toxicity at work makes the workplace less enjoyable. As it increases, top performers who can find better jobs are more tempted to take them, and a company will lose more of its top performers.

Will it affect hiring and training? If employees have a role in hiring and training, why should they hire or train the best available talent if it means they, personally, will fall further in the stacks?

What about the free sharing of information? The more often others fail, the better for an individual, even if it hurts the entire company. And when perceived betrayals occur among employees, they can be paid back with further betrayal.

So by using a zero-sum game to motivate employees to new heights, the entire company becomes less efficient. This is the price of making cooperation too costly. It's an example of a solidarity insanity.

We find them in education when a teacher curves all grades to an artificial number. A curve means the better everyone else does, the worse an individual will do. So instead of groups studying together to master material, they're more likely to work alone. When another student fails, it can cause celebration because it increases everyone else's chances for success. Taken to extremes, this is another type of solidarity insanity.

We find them when we stubbornly disagree with everything an opponent says. It's the delusion that for us to be right, they must be wrong, and the more we agree with them, the more we lose. Instead of progress and understanding, we get entrenchment, embitterment, and an ever-decreasing solidarity. If our goal is to be understood by our opponent and find ways to have more of everything with them, then the inability to look at conflicting facts is a type of solidarity insanity.

In all of these we find common thread. The degree to which we make cooperation costly is the degree to which we support artificial conflict and increase the chance that everyone will lose. These trends struggle to reverse until conflict is made costlier than cooperation. Companies that reward cooperation give their employees better reason to support each other's goals. A classroom based on rewards for helping one another master material gives reasons to celebrate one another's success. Facing ideological opponents with the willingness to listen increases the chance of them hearing us in return.

In short, the opposite of a zero-sum system is of "we all win or lose together" and "the more someone wins, the more we all will win."

Second, insanities occur when we mistake acts of betrayal for acts of group loyalty. For our engineers, loyalty to their cause has, in a series of logical progressions, destroyed progress, made both causes have less of everything, and sabotaged the entire company's future. Each act seems to support their personal group while inadvertently betraying the rest of the employees, their customers, and themselves.

This is the challenge of strong groups. In our example, an individual engineer doesn't have the independence or social support to oppose their group's most destructive decisions. If engineers had more independence from their group, groups wouldn't have had the strength to oppose common sense and work against their own department's goals. There may be a time for strong groups. But when they form, there is danger in them, too.

Third, insanities form when we forget simple truth. Those who promote needless conflict are really betraying everyone for their own gains.

We see this behavior at home, in business, in news, and in politics. To motivate action, someone demonizes their opponent. Maybe it's a news station exaggerating the words of someone it doesn't like. Maybe it's a politician vilifying their rivals by taking their actions out of context. Maybe it's a family member trying to get everyone else to hyperfocus on another's flaws.

When we let solidarity rise for those who promote conflict, we become lost ourselves. Higher solidarity means it's harder to see the problems with their message. It's harder to see their victims as human or hear their pleas for truth. For our engineers, it caused employees to approve of any design of their selected group as long as it opposed the other. This caused deeply flawed products to end up on the market. Like a parasite, the promoters drink nourishment for their selfish causes while their supporters are desiccated.

Why didn't employees fire the betrayers? One reason is lack of awareness. No one knew the depth of the problem until solidarity had blinded too many to one another. If employees were more aware, they'd have choices: (1) continue to support those who propagate the worse conflicts or (2) reject them as the betrayers they really are. However, without awareness, there can be no choice.

This brings us to the <u>fourth point</u>, the need for stabilizing leviathans. A leviathan refers to anything that makes conflict costly. For our engineers, their early leviathan was fear of failure. For a time, this was enough. However, as their company became more stable (a good thing), this leviathan weakened as conflict was no longer seen as too costly (a bad thing). This allowed each group to view their future success as dependent on the other's failure. Nothing punished this. But what could have?

In this employee-owned company, the employees themselves hold the leviathan's power. If enough of them rejected promoters of conflict, the exact leviathan they needed would be reformed. Instead of conflict being accepted, it would be punished with warning, demotion, pay cuts, and dismissal. This would make conflict too costly. It would help transform the support role back into what it's meant to be. Sadly, this hasn't happened, and without it, the company's end seems inevitable. Without strong leviathans, all their hard work will become a footnote in the lexicon of needless human failures.

We've discussed how these concepts apply to business. Now I need to ask you for just a little lenience. This next part is important. I believe it could help us all get more of what we want. However, it's a tricky topic to bring up. Please bear with me for just a little bit as we see these concepts applied to society's biggest arena.

Solidarity and the World

A few years before this book's message had finished focusing, I was invited to speak to a group of Wisconsin state legislators on solidarity as part of a special professional development event. It was a room filled with liberals and conservatives. I spoke with several before and after. They struck me as a group of passionate, intelligent people of different values trying to do what they felt was best for their constituents. This is fortunate since they are arguably part of the most important profession in the country. By their words on a page, industries rise and fall, the unfortunate starve or eat, and injustice is rewarded or punished.

However, the challenges they face are steep. Some of the challenges are solidarity insanities of legendary proportions:

- Political parties have become extremely strong groups, with ardent supporters who want their "side" to win and the other to lose, even if the cost is higher than society can afford.
- Cooperation has become far costlier than conflict. When a politician supports their opponent's values, they risk being misquoted, judged weak, and vilified by their own constituents.
- Public solidarity for politicians is low. While a politician may go into the job to improve society, society's contempt for politicians can turn the most idealistic into the most cynically jaded against the very system they started out excited to improve.

- A surprising amount of a politician's job has become not doing their job but raising money for their party. This is because for their values to be represented, they need the other side to lose more often. This pits an individual's sense of what's right against what's best for their group.
- Even if the public is not on a politician's side, wealthy special interest groups appear to be. By raising solidarity with politicians, a small group with money gains a large amount of political favor they can wield for their own gain.
- News organizations team up with politicians to promote their opponents' worst faults while obscuring their own. By artificially angering the public, they gain the public's attention, support, and revenue. What does the public gain from this deal? Less time, money, understanding, tolerance, and choice.
- Enough public anger can create support for a favored group's most terrible decisions. When these happen, the opportunity cost can be ongoing and catastrophic.

At the time of this book's writing, there have been few examples of a high-ranking politician putting their country ahead of their own group. Each time one has, the politician who did it is often preparing for retirement. When asked if they would have done this if they weren't retiring, the responses are variations of "If I were seeking reelection, I would not have put the country first. I would have put my party first."

Really consider this. When our leaders feel they must put their party's most terrible decisions ahead of what's best for society, we haven't just descended into insanity. We've arrived. If we must feel rage at this, why can't it be for what actually hurts us?

And do you think politicians enjoy being shackled to their party's worse decisions? Do you think they revel in the mind-numbing hours they must spend raising money? Do you think they enjoy slaving away just so one side can gain a new dollop of influence for the next political cycle? Do you think they want to be so misunderstood by a public eager to belittle them?

Don't you think they'd rather be part of accomplishing great things for themselves and the public instead of wasting time over meaningless political inches?

It isn't just public life devastated by an artificial zero-sum system lacking a leviathan.

Can it be fixed? Can we empower our leaders to give everyone more of everything? The solution isn't easy, but it may be simple. What if we do the following?

- Vote for people more interested in cooperation than conflict
- Elect leaders more dedicated to country than ideology
- Stop supporting strong groups when they put their group's values above our own
- Feel more offense when a leader betrays the country in the name of group loyalty
- Hold sources of news accountable when they promote needless conflict in their sale of public poison
- Feel revulsion when politicians actively promote conflict instead of cooperation
- Demand we get more of everything:

- have more fiscal responsibility and decreased taxes through the elimination of needless government waste;
- create better, cheaper, and fairer safety nets that do a better job rejecting freeloaders, offer just what is needed, and use those cost savings to catch more of those who need the most help; and
- have more personal freedom by simplifying outdated regulations that don't prevent major harms

Is having more of everything easy? Of course not. Neither is designing a better computer, medical equipment, airplane, or any other consumer product. Yet we do these all the time. It only happens when enough people work together to get more of everything, including one another's shared values. If we do this, solidarity will rise. When it does, our brain's automatic pathways for understanding, empathy, and civility will open. Instead of a self-propagating conflict of delusion, it would all be different.

Conclusions

How much have we already lost through the world's misunderstanding of solidarity? As we've seen time and again, low solidarity is the pathway of guaranteed future loss. It is the destroyer of our friendships, marriages, careers, and communities. It transforms useless conflict into humanity's destined birthright. It makes continuous self-injury an unavoidable part of living.

Conversely, if solidarity's lessons are correct, then there are higher paths. By aggressively being on another's side, understanding what another values, and supporting another's goals, we can raise solidarity with others. When solidarity rises, it destroys potential conflict, undermines existing hatreds, and reactivates lost empathy. From those, we find our higher paths.

We're limited only by awareness. Without awareness, our only choice is to allow conflicts we don't understand to reach conclusions we can't always afford. However, with awareness, we gain new choices. We realize what happens when cooperation is made too costly. We understand the mechanisms by which misinformation spreads. We learn how supporting other people's values raises solidarity and helps them understand us in return. Through awareness of solidarity, we find ways to have more of everything with those around us.

In short, solidarity helps us take ourselves, the relationships, and the organizations we care about to new heights. It does this by helping us know the true power of our words and actions and gives us better control over the future we want to live in. If just enough people realized solidarity's potential strengths, it could all be different. It could all be better.

Afterword

We've reached the end of this work. The things written here are important to me, and I wish I knew how to better express them. I wish a more talented, better-known writer could have completed this work with improved clarity, charisma, and humor. But they were all (understandably) busy with their own projects, so you've been stuck with me instead. My deepest hope is that some part of this journey has been of value.

As we've seen throughout this work, awareness makes a difference. I believe that just enough awareness from just enough people could change the world in several meaningful ways. However, no one can raise awareness alone. Raising awareness starts with no fewer than two. So if you've found any of these ideas useful, please consider sharing them with others. I'll be there with you, helping how I can.

Solidarity. Noun. Union or fellowship arising from common responsibilities and interests, as among members of a group.

About the Author

A. L. Ranen ("ray-nen") McLanahan started his first job on a floating factory ship in Alaska in the late 1990s. He completed his PhD in Mechanical Engineering in 2011 from Washington State University. After, he kept himself busy with teaching, consultation work, speaking events, and (borderline obsessive) thinking and learning. He is known for his enthusiastic teaching style and fiercely practical methodologies.

He began working on this text in 2013 with the launch of his *McLanahan's Solidarity Project*. This is where the first (and, in his words, most terrible) version of this work was as free seminars and workshops. From 2013-2018, that effort slowly distilled into *The Science of Solidarity*, 2019.

Ranen believes in solidarity's message. If you'd like to support Ranen, see what he's up to, or just drop by and say hi, you can find his website at www.criticalflux.com. He currently lives in the United States in the Midwest with his wife and three children.

References

[1] J. Altman, "How Much Does Employee Turnover Really Cost?," Hiffington Post, 18 January 2017. [Online]. Available: https://www.huffingtonpost.com/entry/how-much-does-employee-turnover-really-cost_us_587fbaf9e4b0474ad4874fb7.

[2] J. K. Maner, C. N. DeWall, R. F. Baumeister and M. Schaller, "Does social exclusion motivate interpersonal reconnection? Resolving the" porcupine problem."," *Journal of personality and social psychology,* vol. 92, no. 1, p. 42, 2007.

[3] "dictionary.com," 21 June 2015. [Online]. Available: http://dictionary.reference.com/browse/solidarity.

[4] J. K. Hamlin, K. Wynn and P. Bloom, "Social evaluation by preverbal infants," *Nature,* vol. 450, no. 7169, pp. 557-559, 2007.

[5] K. D. Kinzler, D. E and S. E. , " The native language of social cognition," *Proceedings of the National Academy of Science,* vol. 104, no. 30, p. 12577–12580, 2007.

[6] J. H. Langlois, L. A. Roggman and L. A. Rieser-Danner, "Infants' differential social responses to attractive and unattractive faces," *Developmental*

Psychology, vol. 26, no. 1, p. 153–159, 1990.

[7] J. Kiley Hamlin, K. Wynn and P. Bloom, "Three-month-olds show a negativity bias in their social evaluations," *Developmental science,* vol. 13, no. 6, pp. 923-929, 2010.

[8] S. O. Lilienfeld and B. P. Andrews, "Development and preliminary validation of a self-report measure of psychopathic personality traits in noncriminal population," *Journal of personality assessment,* vol. 66, no. 3, pp. 488-524, 1996.

[9] H. Larsson, H. Andershed and P. Lichtenstein, "A genetic factor explains most of the variation in the psychopathic personality," *Journal of abnormal psychology,* vol. 115, no. 2, p. 221, 2006.

[10] D. M. Blonigen, B. M. Hicks, R. F. Krueger, C. J. Patrick and W. G. Iacono, "Psychopathic personality traits: Heritability and genetic overlap with internalizing and externalizing psychopathology," *Psychological medicine,* vol. 35, no. 5, pp. 637-648, 2005.

[11] T. Singer, B. Seymour, J. P. O'Doherty, K. E. Stephan, R. J. Dolan and C. D. Frith, "Empathic neural responses are modulated by the perceived fairness of others," *Nature,* vol. 439, no. 7075, pp. 466-469, 2006.

[12] R. R. Provine, Laughter: A scientific investigation,

Penguin, 2001.

[13] B. Burr, "Why Do I Do This," 22 December 2012. [Online]. Available: https://www.youtube.com/watch?v=Iynom7gdeNc.

[14] S. Andrews and I. Harris, "Ian Harris: The Skeptic Comedian," 18 March 2018. [Online]. Available: http://www.thethinkingatheist.com/podcast/ian-harris-the-skeptic-comedian.

[15] D. Baer, "This Cognitive Bias Explains Why Pretty People Make 12% More Money Than Everybody Else," 4 11 2014. [Online]. Available: http://www.businessinsider.com/halo-effect-money-beauty-bias-2014-11.

[16] N. J. Salkind and K. Rasmussen, Encyclopedia of Educational Psychology, Volume 1, SAGE, 2008.

[17] J. J. a. S. J. C. Gunnell, "When emotionality trumps reason: A study of individual processing style and juror bias 28.6 (2010): 850-877.," *Behavioral Sciences & the Law,* vol. 28, no. 6, pp. 850-877, 2010.

[18] F. W. J. A. G. a. L. M. C. Schneider, "Social psychological theory," *Applied social psychology 2nd ed.,* 2012.

[19] E. L. Thorndike, "A constant error in psychological ratings," *Journal of applied psychology,* vol. 4, no. 1, pp. 25-29, 1920.

[20] A. Laub, "As It Happens: Pacific Crest Trail," As It Happens Creative, 3 May 2014. [Online]. Available: http://www.asithappens.tv/new-page/.

[21] S. Han, Y. Fan, X. Xu, J. Qin, B. Wu, X. Wang and L. Mao, "Empathic neural responses to others' pain are modulated by emotional contexts," *Human brain mapping*, vol. 10, no. 3227-3237, p. 30, 2009.

[22] J. Rifkin, "RSA ANIMATE: The Empathic Civilisation," 6 May 2010. [Online]. Available: https://www.youtube.com/watch?v=l7AWnfFRc7g.

[23] M. L. Meyer, C. L. Masten, Y. Ma, C. Wang, Z. Shi, N. I. Eisenberger and S. Han, "Empathy for the social suffering of friends and strangers recruits distinct patterns of brain activation," *Social Cognitive and Affective Neuroscience,* vol. 8, no. 1, p. 446–454, 2013.

[24] L. R. Tropp and T. F. Pettigrew, "How does intergroup contact reduce prejudice? Meta-analytic tests of three mediators," *European Journal of Social Psychology,* vol. 38, p. 922–934, 2008.

[25] C. D. Batson, D. A. Lishner, J. Cook and S. Sawyer, "Similarity and Nurturance: Two Possible Sources of Empathy for Strangers," *Basic and Applied Social Psychology,* vol. 27, no. 1, p. 15–25, 2005.

[26] L. Morales, "Knowing Someone Gay/Lesbian Affects Views of Gay Issues," Gallup, 29 May 2009. [Online]. Available:

http://news.gallup.com/poll/118931/knowing-someone-gay-lesbian-affects-views-gay-issues.aspx.

[27] N. I. Eisenberger, M. D. Lieberman and K. D. Williams, "Does Rejection Hurt? An fMRI Study of Social Exclusion," *Science,* vol. 302, no. 290, pp. 290-292, 2003.

[28] A. W. Gouldner, "The Norm of Reciprocity: A Preliminary Statement," *America Sociological Review,* vol. 25, pp. 161-178, 1960.

[29] E. Fehr and S. Gachter, "Fairness and Retaliation: The Economics of Reciprocity," *Journal of Economic Perspectives,* vol. 14, no. 3, p. 159–181, 2000.

[30] D. B. Strohmetz, B. Rind, R. Fisher and M. Lynn, "Using Candy to Increase Tips," *Journal of Applied Social Psychology,* vol. 32, pp. 300-309, 2002.

[31] A. H. Bartlett, The man who loved books too much: the true story of a thief, a detective, and a world of literary obsession, Penguin, 2009.

[32] C. M. Kujawa, "Before 'raw water,' radium water was the craze — and then people died," Chicago Tribune, 3 March 2018. [Online]. Available: http://www.chicagotribune.com/news/opinion/commentary/ct-perspec-flash-radium-elixir-fad-cure-cocktails-0304-20180220-story.html.

[33] T. Gray, "For that Healthy Glow, Drink Radiation!,"

Popular Science, 17 August 2004. [Online]. Available: https://www.popsci.com/scitech/article/2004-08/healthy-glow-drink-radiation.

[34] "The Element Radium," Jefferson Lab, [Online]. Available: https://education.jlab.org/itselemental/ele088.html.

[35] S. Illing, "This is what love does to your brain," Vox, 23 April 2018. [Online]. Available: https://www.vox.com/science-and-health/2018/4/23/17247932/love-sex-science-marriage-psychology-brain.

The following sources influenced this work but weren't explicitly referenced in this work's final form.

[36] "Brain Anatomy," 8 July 2015. [Online]. Available: http://www.princetonbrainandspine.com/subject.php?pn=brain-anatomy-066.

[37] R. F. &. L. M. R. Baumeister, "The Need to Belong: Desire for Interpersonal Attachments as a Fundamental Human Motivation.," *Psychological Bulletin,* pp. 497-529, 1995.

[38] J. M. Twenge, R. F. Baumeister, C. N. DeWall, N. J. Ciarocco and J. M. Bartels, "Social exclusion decreases prosocial behavior," *Journal of personality and social psychology,* vol. 92, no. 1, p. 56, 2007.

[39] J. M. Twenge, K. R. Catanese and R. F. Baumeister,

"Social exclusion causes self-defeating behavior," *Journal of personality and social psychology,* vol. 83, no. 3, p. 606, 2002.

[40] R. F. Baumeister and M. R. Leary, "The Need to Belong: Desire for Interpersonal Attachments as a Fundamental Human Motivation," *Psychological Bulletin,* vol. 117, no. 3, pp. 497-529, 1995.

[41] J. E. Maddux, L. W. Norton and M. R. Leary, "Cognitive components of social anxiety: An investigation of the integration of self-presentation theory and self-efficacy theory," *ournal of Social and Clinical Psychology,* vol. 6, no. 2, pp. 180-190, 1988.

[42] . C.-Q. Lai, "How much of human height is genetic and how much is due to nutrition?," *Scientific American,* 2006.

[43] G. Carnac, S. Ricaud, B. Vernus and A. Bonnieu , "Myostatin: biology and clinical relevance," *Mini Reviews in Medicinal Chemistry,* vol. 6, no. 7, p. 765–70, 2006.

[44] N. Kanwisher, J. McDermott and M. M. Chun, "The fusiform face area: a module in human extrastriate cortex specialized for face perception.," *The Journal of Neuroscience,* vol. 16, no. 11, pp. 4302-4311, 1997.

[45] D. Cordes and e. al., "Mapping Functionally Related Regions of Brain with Functional Connectivity MR Imaging," *Mapping functionally related regions of brain with*

functional connectivity MR *imaging,* vol. 21, no. 9, pp. 1636-1644, 2000.

[46] L. J. Buxbaum and H. B. Coslett, "Specialised structural descriptions for human body parts: Evidence from autotopagnosi," *Cognitive Neuropsychology,* vol. 18, no. 4, pp. 289-306, 2001.

[47] A. Raine, The anatomy of violence: The biological roots of crime, Pantheon Books, 2013.

[48] R. Kanai and e. al., "Political orientations are correlated with brain structure in young adults."," *Current Biology,* vol. 21, no. 8, pp. 677-680, 2011.

[49] P. M. Thompson and e. al., "Genetic influences on brain structure," *Nature neuroscience,* vol. 4, no. 12, pp. 1253-1258, 2001.

[50] J. S. Peper and e. al., "Genetic influences on human brain structure: a review of brain imaging studies in twins," *Human Brain Mapping,* vol. 28, no. 6, pp. 464-473, 2007.

[51] A. Tellegen and e. al., "Personality similarity in twins reared apart and together," *Journal of personality and social psychology,* vol. 54, no. 6, p. 1031, 1988.

[52] A. J. Stunkard and e. al., "The body-mass index of twins who have been reared apart," *New England Journal of Medicine,* vol. 322, no. 21, pp. 1483-1487, 1990.

[53] D. Knoch and e. al., "Diminishing reciprocal fairness by disrupting the right prefrontal cortex," *Science,* vol. 314, no. 5800, pp. 829-832, 2006.

[54] A. M. Hull, "Neuroimaging findings in post-traumatic stress disorder Systematic review," *The British Journal of Psychiatry,* vol. 181, no. 2, pp. 102-110, 2002.

[55] S. L. Rauch and e. al., "Exaggerated amygdala response to masked facial stimuli in posttraumatic stress disorder: a functional MRI study," *Biological psychiatry,* vol. 47, no. 9, pp. 769-776, 2000.

[56] R. A. Bryant, "Amygdala and ventral anterior cingulate activation predicts treatment response to cognitive behaviour therapy for post-traumatic stress disorder," *Psychological medicine,* vol. 38, no. 4, pp. 555-561, 2008.

[57] E. Luders, A. W. Toga, N. Lepore and C. Gaser, "The underlying anatomical correlates of long-term meditation: larger hippocampal and frontal volumes of gray matter," *Neuroimage,* vol. 45, no. 3, pp. 672-678, 2009.

[58] B. K. Hölzel, J. Carmody, M. Vangel, C. Congleton, S. M. Yerramsetti, T. Gard and S. W. Lazar, "Mindfulness practice leads to increases in regional brain gray matter density. Psychiatry Research," *Neuroimaging,* vol. 191, no. 1, pp. 36-43, 2011.

[59] G. Pagnoni and M. Cekic, "Age effects on gray matter volume and attentional performance in Zen meditation.," *Neurobiology of aging,* vol. 28, no. 10, pp. 1623-1627, 2007.

[60] P. Gilbert, "The evolution of social attractiveness and its role in shame, humiliation, guilt and therapy," *British Journal of Medical Psychology,* vol. 70, no. 2, pp. 113-147, 1997.

[61] P. Gilbert and M. T. McGuire, Shame, status, and social roles: Psychobiology and evolution. Shame: Interpersonal behavior, psychopathology, and culture, 1998, pp. 99-125.

[62] C. Boehm, Moral origins: The evolution of virtue, altruism, and shame, Basic Books, 2012.

[63] J. L. Tracy and D. Matsumoto, "The spontaneous expression of pride and shame: Evidence for biologically innate nonverbal displays," *Proceedings of the National Academy of Sciences,* vol. 105, no. 33, pp. 11655-11660, 2008.

[64] S. H. Schwartz and W. Bilsky, "Toward a theory of the universal content and structure of values: Extensions and cross-cultural replications," *Journal of personality and social psychology,* vol. 58, no. 5, 1990.

[65] D. J. Bolger, C. A. Perfetti and W. Schneider, "Cross-cultural effect on the brain revisited: Universal structures plus writing system variation," *Human brain*

mapping, vol. 25, no. 1, pp. 92-104, 2005.

[66] J. Haidt, "The emotional dog and its rational tail: a social intuitionist approach to moral judgment," *Psychological review,* vol. 108, no. 4, p. 814, 2001.

[67] J. Haidt, The righteous mind: Why good people are divided by politics and religion, Vintage, 2012.

[68] N. Khatri and H. A. Ng, "The role of intuition in strategic decision making," *Human relations,* vol. 53, no. 1, pp. 57-86, 2000.

[69] M. H. Raidl and T. I. Lubart, "An empirical study of intuition and creativity," *Imagination, Cognition and Personality,* vol. 20, no. 3, pp. 217-230, 2001.

[70] H. T. Reis, S. M. Smith, C. L. Carmichael, P. A. Caprariello, F. F. Tsai, A. Rodrigues and M. R. Maniaci, "Are you happy for me? How sharing positive events with others provides personal and interpersonal benefits," *Journal of personality and social psychology,* vol. 99, no. 2, p. 311, 2010.

[71] D. J. Nutt, "Relationship of neurotransmitters to the symptoms of major depressive disorder," *The Journal of clinical psychiatry,* vol. 69, pp. 4-7, 2007.

[72] G. &. B. V. Di Chiara, "Reward system and addiction: what dopamine does and doesn't do.," *Current opinion in pharmacology,* vol. 7, no. 1, pp. 69-76, 2007.

[73] P. H. S. J. R. U. &. E. U. Wirtz, "Higher overcommitment to work is associated with lower norepinephrine secretion before and after acute psychosocial stress in men.," *Psychoneuroendocrinology,* vol. 33, no. 1, pp. 92-99, 2008.

[74] M. Stout, he sociopath next door: The ruthless versus the rest of us, Harmony Books, 2006.

[75] K. Arrow, Discrimination in the Labour Market, Oxford: Oxford University Press., 1980.